8 Steps to Better Security

A Simple Cyber Resilience Guide for Business

Kim Crawley

WILEY

Published by John Wiley & Sons, Inc., Hoboken, New Jersey.
Published simultaneously in Canada.

978-1-119-81123-7
978-1-119-81125-1 (ebk.)
978-1-119-81124-4 (ebk.)

For general information on our other products and services or for technical support, please contact our Customer Care Department within the United States at (800) 762-2974, outside the United States at (317) 572-3993 or fax (317) 572-4002.

Wiley also publishes its books in a variety of electronic formats. Some content that appears in print may not be available in electronic formats. For more information about Wiley products, visit our web site at www.wiley.com.

Library of Congress Control Number: 2021942648

Cover image: © Zhenjin Li/Getty Images
Cover design: Wiley

SKY10029017_081221

To Jay for loving me.
To the Smith (Smith-Collins) clan for giving me a new family.
To Tori for upholding the responsibility of being the last Crawley in my life.
To Kate Brew, Joe Pettit, David Turner, Haris Pylarinos, Aris Zikopoulos, Daphne Deiktaki, Kate Bevan, and Phil Wylie for the professional opportunities you've granted me.

About the Author

Kim has been a prolific cybersecurity researcher and writer for well over a decade. Her years spent with BlackBerry Cylance, AT&T Cybersecurity, Venafi, and several other cybersecurity industry leaders gave her a thorough perspective on enterprise cybersecurity needs and trends. Years of friendships with CISOs, malware researchers, cyber threat intel specialists, and network administrators have provided her valuable insight to the scary ways the cyber threat landscape is evolving. Currently, Kim is focused on running Hack The Box's new blog, writing books about practical cybersecurity knowledge, and doing a little bit of dark web OSINT for a major Canadian bank on the side.

Acknowledgments

To my loving partner, Jay Smith, for all the times you've bragged about your "brilliant cybersecurity hacker girlfriend" to your family and your buddies. We're three years together, going strong! Let's make it three decades.

To my late father, Michael Crawley, for teaching me how to write for a living, from my toddler years to my twenties. It's a shame you didn't live long enough to witness my success.

To my publisher, Jim Minatel, for believing in my wacky ideas, and to my editor, Robyn Alvarez, for her patience with my eccentricities.

All the soft animals in my bed are also very much loved and appreciated.

Contents

Foreword

I first met Kim Crawley in person in October 2019, in Toronto at SecTor, Canada's version of DEFCON. We'd been acquainted for a long time via Twitter, and she was the one who originally turned me onto SecTor and inspired me to submit a talk, citing the merits of her hometown and the conference. She was right about both. In between the superb sessions there, amidst the fantastic energy of that conference and the international vibe of the city, we walked around and talked about information security, cyber resilience, and neurodiversity, topics woven deeply into the fabric of both our lives. Over lunch one afternoon, our conversation came around to how our industry can do a better job of helping small and midsize organizations better prepare for strategic response to cybercrime. We agreed that by helping smaller and more vulnerable organizations, the larger organizations and the collective industry as a whole would also benefit. We compared notes on tactics and strategies that don't have to cost a lot of time or money.

Shortly after our time and discussions at SecTor, Covid-19 hit. Kim didn't slow down. She founded DisInfoSec, a pop-up infosec conference showcasing infosec professionals who identify as neurodivergent (including ADD, AHDH, autism, Asperger's, dyslexia, and more). Inspired by Lesley Carhart's PancakesCon and other events, DisInfoSec was a first-of-its-kind event and took place on July 11, 2020. The con included a lot of great talks and raised funds for the Autistic Self Advocacy Network, the Autistic Women and Nonbinary Network, and the Council of Canadians with Disabilities. Kim's commitment to improving inclusion and nudging the world to a better place is showcased in her actions, and this new book is merely an extension of her productive mindset.

If you're new to Kim's work, her past and present articles on infosec and cyber for AT&T Cybersecurity, Cylance, and others are some of the most accessible to read, especially for anyone who is new to those topics. Kim writes with spirit and an intimate awareness of the diverse audiences who may be reading, which makes her style a stand-out. Her new book is no exception: *8 Steps to Better Security: A Simple Cyber Resilience Guide for Business* is an easy read for first-timers, seasoned veterans, and anyone else keen to learn more about infosec and cyber resilience using practical, quick-win steps you can take right away to better prepare your organization for a strategic response to unplanned events that would otherwise compromise your productivity, reputation, and bottom line. That's real peace of mind, and I don't know about you, but these days I'll take all of that I can get. Enjoy the book!

Chad Calease

Chief Information Security Officer

`https://resilience.sh`

Introduction

Pandora's box has been opened. Businesses in all industries run on computer data, and now there's no turning back.

When I was little, offices were still full of filing cabinets. Each customer, patient, client, vendor, and supplier had their own labeled manila folder in one of those cabinets. In fact, many offices have kept their filing cabinets well into the 21st century. Spilling your coffee on a few forms could damage lucrative business data. Unauthorized data access happened if someone found the secretary's physical key and unlocked cabinets they weren't entitled to. Some cabinets were designed to be fire resistant. But backing up all that data to a second location for the sake of business continuity in a disaster is always a good idea, one that was often not conducted because a clerk would have to put each page through the photo copier one by one, ever so tediously.

Now businesses keep their lucrative data on computers, whether that business is Smith's Convenience on the street corner or a multibillion-dollar military contractor. Some of these businesses still have filing cabinets, but they're working hard to digitize as much as possible.

The computer data that flows through businesses in all industries isn't just sensitive data on customers. It isn't all precious financial data, either. Some of it is security patches for our operating systems, applications, and firmware. Some of it is the email your employees are sending and receiving, whether on a company-owned PC or on their phone wherever they are. Some of it even keeps devices in the office running—your smart thermostats and your internet-connected heart monitors.

Keeping all the data that flows through your business secure is absolutely vital. Otherwise, a cybercriminal could steal your trade secrets or your clients' credit card data. Or they could perform a distributed denial-of-service attack on your production systems. Or they could infect your whole network with ransomware, both on the premises and on the cloud. Your company can be liable for any sensitive data that's stolen, especially if it results in your customers and vendors being harmed. And if your production systems face even a couple of hours of downtime, your business could lose millions in productivity. Chances are there are data privacy and security regulations that also apply to your business, and you could face hefty fines for security incidents and noncompliance. Often, fines can be in the millions under laws such as the European Union's General Data Protection Regulation.

A few hundred thousand dollars spent on improving your security will likely save your business millions of dollars in the long run. But simply spending money isn't enough. You need to spend it wisely, and you need to work on security every day. As cybersecurity expert Bruce Schneier says, "Security is a process, not a product."

I have spent the past several years researching and writing about cybersecurity for business on behalf of many major tech brands, such as AT&T Cybersecurity, Venafi, BlackBerry Cylance, Comodo, and Sophos. And every day I work, I have discussions with people who directly work on improving the security of businesses of all sizes and in a wide variety of industries.

I know it can be overwhelming when people are tasked with improving their company's cybersecurity. Where do you start? More importantly, how do you convince your executives that having a decent security budget and hiring security professionals is important? It's a struggle many people around the world face all the time.

I'm a regular computer security geek. But I've been adjacent to businesspeople my whole life. My (now retired) mother went from working in payroll to being a human resources director and vice president for Bayerische Landesbank back when they had a Toronto branch in the 1990s. I have friends who work as equity traders for companies like Manulife Financial. More importantly, I'm friends with many chief information security officers (CISOs).

So, I'm a geek and a "creative class" person according to Richard Florida. But although I don't fit in with the suits on Bay Street and Wall Street, I know how they think. I know what makes them tick: money, of course!

Ultimately, applying the advice in this book will cost you money, but it will save your business a lot more money over time. Spend $1 now to prevent losing $10 in the future. Think beyond next quarter's profits! Security-harden your business for the years ahead.

I'm going to be honest with you. Looking at the business bestsellers often makes me cringe. I distrust all books that say they're going to make me rich. I'm not an individualist-capitalist (I don't have any capital!); I believe in society, and I believe we're all interdependent. I think some of your success is in your hands, but a lot of your fate is in the hands of other people. I strongly believe that absolutely no one is "self-made."

I pride myself in sharing honest and useful information with the world, not tips on how to leverage market disruption for maximum capital gains, or whatever. I might as well tell you a 100 percent cabbage soup diet will make you permanently skinny and cure all disease on Earth. Honestly, my conscience doesn't feel good about that stuff. This book is for businesspeople, whether you wear a Brooks Brothers suit or a Lacoste polo shirt and khakis or a hard hat and overalls or jeans and a T-shirt. Cyber threats are bad now, and they'll only get worse. Make sure your business thrives in the ever-evolving cyber threat landscape with the eight steps in this book.

That's what I love to do: take useful information, share it in simple language, and break it down into manageable little bites. This book won't make your brain hurt. You can read one chapter at a time, or even just a few pages at a time, and glean useful insight that you can use in your everyday lives—as long as working in a business is part of your everyday life.

This book is based on the research I've done and knowledge I've acquired through years of work as a cybersecurity news and information scribe. And my knowledge is augmented with the insight of many of the world's top CISOs and other business leaders in security. It was a great pleasure for me to interview all these people and pick their brains a little bit for your benefit. This book is further enhanced with the findings of business security research studies and the aftermath of some of the most notable business security incidents. Mistakes become valuable when we make sure we learn from them!

Let's summarize the topics I cover in this book. Chapters 1 through 8 cover what this book is all about: *8 Steps to Better Security*. Each of those chapters is one of those steps. Chapter 9 will show you how to put it all together.

Chapter 1, "Step 1: Foster a Strong Security Culture": This is where everything starts—not with an audit or a security budget, but with how to make sure everyone in your organization takes security seriously, from your janitor to your CEO. Policy is vital, but it's useful only if it influences people's behavior. The best information security policies in the world become ineffective if people don't abide by them and enforce them. I'm fascinated by psychology and sociology, and these areas are a lot more important to cybersecurity than laypeople assume. This chapter will explain how you can begin to foster a strong security culture, whether you're a new startup or a 50-year-old company. If you do something more than three times, it'll become a habit. Making sure your habits and attitudes are good will set the foundation for everything your business does with regard to cybersecurity. Effective information security is paramount in the 21st century, regardless of your company's industry or size. So, let's get off to the best possible start. This chapter will show you how.

Chapter 2, "Step 2: Build a Security Team": If your company is medium-sized or larger, you'll benefit from having staff who work on cybersecurity as their full-time job. If your company is smaller, your one to five IT specialists will need to be tasked to manage your business's information security, even if your IT specialist is the nerd who comes into your little shop once a week to make sure your point-of-sale works properly. How your company builds a security team will vary according to your size and industry. The principles and advice in this chapter are designed to be useful for businesses of all kinds. The buck must stop somewhere. Make sure the buck stops with people who are ready to security-harden your company and rise to the challenge of any potential security incidents. This chapter includes tips on what sort of experience and credentials people should have in particular roles, so you can hire and delegate intelligently

Chapter 3, "Step 3: Regulatory Compliance": In business-speak, this is a major "pain point" for most companies. Pretty much all companies of all sizes and in all industries must comply with your region's general data privacy regulations. On top of that, if your company is in the medical field, there are usually regulations specific to healthcare data that must be complied with. If your company is in finance, there are usually financial-sector data privacy regulations as well. On top of that, if your company is in or deals with the public sector, there is often another whole set of regulations that are also crucial to abide by. Some audits are random and unpredictable, some may be scheduled, and some may occur in response to a data breach or similar incident. This chapter will help you take an inventory of which specific regulations apply to your business. From there, I offer tips to help you make sure you're set up for compliance so your business can continue to comply every day your business operates. Cybersecurity experts debate over how useful regulations are when it comes to preventing or mitigating security incidents. But we all agree that compliance is a must because the hefty fines for violations can really hurt your bottom line. The reputation damage can be immense too. Customers and clients need to feel that you take the security of their data seriously if they're going to be comfortable with spending money on your company's products and services.

Chapter 4, "Step 4: Frequent Security Testing": You absolutely cannot know how well secured your company's networks, computers, and applications are without frequent security testing. Having your assets security tested isn't simply a matter of emailing a third-party security firm and saying, "I need a security test." Cybersecurity testing comes in many different forms. The kind of testing you need will vary according to many different factors, including but not limited to the types of networks you have, how large they are, and which industry your business is in. So, knowing where to start when it comes to security testing will take this entire chapter, at the least. But don't be dismayed. This book is designed for businesspeople, not computer nerds. By the time you're done reading the chapter, you'll be ready to initiate the security testing your company needs in order to face the ever-evolving cyber threat landscape with confidence. The security testing your company needs can be a combination of internal red team specialists and third-party penetration testers. They may need to test once per year or every time your network changes in a significant way. Don't know what a red team or penetration testing is? Then this chapter is definitely for you!

Chapter 5, "Step 5: Security Framework Application": A cybersecurity framework is a set of standards that companies can base their security policies and procedures on. The most popular cybersecurity frameworks focus on how your business should prepare for and respond to cybersecurity incidents. Often companies can choose which framework is most useful for their organization. Unlike security regulation compliance, using a cybersecurity framework is optional, but highly recommended nonetheless. Also, unlike security regulation compliance, cybersecurity frameworks aren't usually tied to a particular state, province, or nation. The same frameworks are used by organizations around the world in many different countries and industries.

The NIST Cybersecurity Framework is the most widely implemented framework, and other frameworks have been inspired by it. Some of the other frameworks I cover in this chapter include ISO 27000 Cybersecurity Framework Series, CIS Cybersecurity Framework, and COBIT Cybersecurity Framework. I explain the basics of each of these frameworks and share what cybersecurity experts believe are their strengths and weaknesses. No matter what, though, your organization must have policies and procedures for preparing for and responding to security incidents. With proper preparation, cyber incidents will do much less harm to your organization, and you will save money in the long run.

Chapter 6, "Step 6: Control Your Data Assets": Every bit of your organization's data is stored on at least one computing device. Whether your network is on the premises, on the cloud, or on a hybrid network. Whether your company has a bring-your-own-device policy or not. Whether your workers work in the corporate office or from their homes. Your organization must first determine where all of your data resides, how it's transmitted, and which entities own the devices, and then design policies and procedures for securing all of those devices.

These data assets not only contain intellectual property and sensitive data (such as login credentials and financial information), but also keep your business running each and every day. A retail business needs a constantly operating point-of-sale system. An online service needs an always-working web application. A dental practice needs their radiography machines to always work, and so on. Computers with downtime result in lots of lost revenue and customers. Your organization needs to fully understand and control all of your data assets to protect them from cyber incidents.

Chapter 7, "Step 7: Understand the Human Factor": Many laypeople believe that successful cyberattacks require intense computer wizardry from cyberattackers, but the sad truth is that most cyber incidents, including the most destructive attacks, involve social engineering at one point or another. Fooling the people within your organization who have access to your computer systems is the most common way that cyber threat actors gain unlawful entry into your organization's networks. Phishing is a primary means of social engineering exploits. What is phishing? Phishing is when a threat actor uses a web page, text message, email, or social media post to imitate a trusted entity, such as a bank, a utility company, the government, or a well-known business. Even us cybersecurity professionals sometimes succumb to phishing attacks. We must never get overconfident. This chapter will cover how employees and contractors should be trained to prevent phishing attacks, as well as how to prevent other social engineering attacks, such as downloading Trojan malware. This chapter is also designed to consider how organizations have evolved during the Covid-19 pandemic to support many employees and contractors working from home for the first time.

Chapter 8, "Step 8: Build Redundancy and Resilience": Any cyber incident or technical glitch that causes network downtime hurts your business's productivity. That loss of productivity has an immediate impact on your bottom line. Here's how to design networks with redundant capacity through the power of the cloud, how to properly back up your data and applications from threats like ransomware, and how to design hot sites and cold sites for business continuity in the face of potential disasters. Your organization needs backed-up data and extra computers to survive the cyber threats that can impact any entity.

Once we cover all eight steps, we finish with Chapter 9, "Afterword." I have advice for implementing all eight of these steps. But my knowledge is augmented with tips from some of the world's top business cybersecurity professionals. So, as you prepare to improve the cybersecurity of your organization, you'll benefit from an amalgam of the best advice available.

Congratulations, you're ready to prepare your company for the evolving cyber threat landscape, no matter which country or industry you're in or the size of your business! Pat yourself on the back and then get to work. You can do it. I believe in you.

Chapter 1
Step 1: Foster a Strong Security Culture

People generally assume that cybersecurity is a technological area of study and take it for granted that cyber threat actors, called *hackers* by laypeople, must be computer geniuses. They have to have some mastery of computer programming code and an advanced understanding of how computer networks work. And if you take the Hollywood stereotype really seriously, then you probably believe that the most notorious cyberattackers work from an elaborate computer lab in their mom's basement, wearing a hoodie and typing at 400 words per minute. I imagine something like the movie *War Games*, but with a more 21st century–style presentation.

So, surely, if you're learning about cybersecurity, it's all about computer science stuff, right? You likely bought this book because you're a businessperson who wants to improve the security posture of your company. So, maybe you expect this book is about hiring the right supernerds for your IT department, and then you just let them do their technical wizardry. Why do you need eight steps for that? Step 1: hire computer experts. Step 2: don't think about cybersecurity ever again.

Actually, it's not that simple. Understanding computer technology is definitely a big part of understanding cybersecurity. But cybersecurity also overlaps with the arts and humanities. To understand cybersecurity properly, you must learn about the psychology of the interactions of people with computers. Then you must also learn the sociology of the interactions of groups of people with computers and how people within those groups influence each other's behavior. *Cybersecurity is as much of a human area of study as it is a technological area of study.*

The first step to improving your company's security posture is to foster a strong security culture. Culture doesn't manifest in the firmware code on your PC's motherboard. Culture is about the ideas, attitudes, and styles people create and maintain in their interactions with each other. Your company could have the best security policies and the most expensive network security devices. But if the people in your company don't behave in a secure way, improving your security posture will be an uphill battle.

From the balcony of my skyscraper condominium, I can see mighty maple trees thriving near Toronto's lakeshore. Those maple trees evolved over thousands of years to survive harsh Canadian winters. Their genes make them hardy, and they produce a resilient life-form. But if it weren't for the deep nutritious soil and sufficient annual precipitation in their environment, those maple trees wouldn't be able to grow and survive for hundreds of years. That's why you don't see maple trees growing in the desert.

Your company's security culture needs to be the nutritious soil and sufficient precipitation for the seeds and saplings of your computer hardware, software, networking, security policies, and security staff to thrive to become the hardy maple trees of a resilient business with a strong security posture. Even though I don't intend for this to be a cheesy self-help book, I'm not going to stop with the flowery analogies. So, just hang on for the ride!

Before I get further into explaining how to foster a strong security culture, I really need you to understand how important psychology and sociology are to cybersecurity. So, I will start with a really abridged version of the story of Kevin Mitnick, the man who may still be the world's most infamous cyberattacker.

Kevin Mitnick, Human Hacker Extraordinaire

Kevin Mitnick is so notorious that you've likely heard of him, even if you've never taken an interest in cybersecurity. His name was mentioned in news headlines in the 1980s and 1990s.

Mitnick is known for conducting two major cyberattacks. The first one was in the news throughout the 1980s: a penetration of Digital Equipment Corporation's (DEC's) network, called The Ark. DEC was a major manufacturer of computer hardware and developer of computer software from the 1960s to the 1990s, focused on the enterprise market. It was perhaps best known for its PDP line of minicomputers. The minicomputers of the era were definitely not "mini" by today's standards. Early PDP hardware consisted of large boxes the size of a few refrigerators stacked together. Even the later PDP models produced in the 1970s were at least the size of a single refrigerator. They were classified as minicomputers simply because they didn't require the space of multiple rooms of a building. Anyway, I'm going to refrain from rambling on and on about the history of computing. Just understand that PDP computers are very important when it came to large businesses being able to process thousands or millions of customer records, in areas such as the airline industry or public utility companies. This was the most frequent way computers were used in the years before PCs (known as *microcomputers*) entered most people's homes.

In late 1979, a teenaged Kevin Mitnick acquired access to DEC's own computer system that he was not permitted to have. This was widely reported in the news during his criminal trial in the 1980s.

Mitnick intended to describe how he maliciously accessed DEC's computer system in his book, *The Art of Deception*, published by my own book's publisher, John Wiley & Sons, in 2002. This material didn't end up in the first edition of Mitnick's book, but he confirmed to *Wired* that he wrote this:

> Claiming to be Anton Chernoff, one of the (DEC) project's lead developers, I placed a simple phone call to the system manager. I claimed I couldn't log in to one of "my" accounts and was convincing enough to talk the guy into giving me access and allowing me to select a password of my choice.

Something stands out to me here. Without an account name and password, he wouldn't have been able to get in. The way he acquired those credentials was by social engineering. *Social engineering* in a cybersecurity context is all about fooling human beings into helping you acquire access to computer systems you aren't allowed to have. The specific kind of social engineering Mitnick did is called *vishing*. Vishing is when someone uses phone calls to pretend to be a trusted party, such as DEC developer Anton Chernoff, to acquire information that you're not entitled to have and that you can use to facilitate a cyberattack. Vishing is a category of phishing, where media such as text messages, web pages, emails, or social media messages are used to impersonate trusted entities to acquire malicious computer access. All kinds of phishing, including vishing, are common types of social engineering attacks. Mitnick exploited human psychology. *The Art of Deception*, indeed.

Mitnick started to learn social engineering when he was really young. In the mid-1970s when he was 12, he wanted to be able to ride Los Angeles public transit for free. So, he dumpster dived for unused bus transfer slips. He tricked a bus driver into giving him a ticket punch by saying he needed it for a school project. From there, young Kevin Mitnick was able to spoof bus transfers for free rides. But he couldn't do it without social engineering the bus driver.

Mitnick's successful Los Angeles bus exploit gave him the confidence to attempt social engineering in other ways. He went on to trick his way into DEC's computer system. After years of criminal investigations and a trial, he was convicted in 1988 and sentenced to a year in prison and three years of supervised release. By the early 1990s, toward the end of his supervised release, he conducted his second notorious cyberattack.

Mitnick social engineered his way into the voicemail system of Pacific Bell, a major telecommunications company in California. His techniques were very similar to how he penetrated DEC. Those in the know didn't consider Mitnick to be a master of computer science; rather, he was a clever conman. Eventually, Mitnick targeted an actual computer science master, Tsutomu Shimomura.

Shimomura studied physics with the famous physicist Richard Feynman before he pursued computer technology research at San Diego Supercomputer Center full time. Mitnick wanted access to Shimomura's work. He chose the wrong target this time, because Shimomura helped law enforcement investigate Mitnick's Pacific Bell breach and other criminal activities. The FBI arrested Mitnick in 1995, and he was in prison until 2000.

From there, Mitnick decided to use his skills in law-abiding ways. He wrote books, some of which were published by Wiley. And he also started his own cybersecurity firm, Mitnick Security Consulting, LLC.

The Importance of a Strong Security Culture

The cyber threat actors who will try to harm your company could be just glorified conmen like Mitnick or brilliant computer scientists like Shimomura. Either way, the majority of cyberattacks involve social engineering at one point or another. A strong security culture hardens against social engineering exploits by making your employees, contractors, and executives less likely to succumb to them. A strong security culture also encourages your workers to develop good habits in the ways that they use computer technology, so your precious data assets are better protected.

A strong security culture doesn't stop at your IT department. Everyone from the janitors to the CEO must be a part of it because computer systems aren't used only by people with IT certifications. Even an authorized person entering your office could put your computer networks at risk.

One of the most important things you can do to make sure your company can thrive in our rapidly evolving cyber threat landscape is to establish and maintain a strong security culture. And that's what step 1 is all about. With this crucial step taken care of, the other seven steps in my book will be feasible. For a cybersecure business, start with people's behaviors and attitudes.

Let's start by demystifying the word *hacker*, shall we?

Hackers Are the Bad Guys, Right?

When most people hear the word *hacker*, they think of cybercriminals. Apparently, hackers are the bad guys. This is a misconception that's not only reinforced in Hollywood movies and TV shows but also in the news. When cyberattacks are covered in TV news shows, newspapers, magazines, and online news sources, the bad guys who perpetrate the crimes are called *hackers*. Those of us who promote a more accurate use of the word face an uphill battle with the public consciousness.

One of my favorite books of all time is Steven Levy's *Hackers*. It was published by Dell, Penguin, and O'Reilly in various editions between 1984 and 2010. That book is one of the best ways to learn about the history of actual computer hackers, beginning with the first proper electronic computer, ENIAC, deployed in 1948. Levy covers the history of hacking from the 1950s onward.

Hackers are people who find new and innovative ways to use computer technology. Some of the people who became famous billionaires in the tech industry, such as Steve Wozniak, Steve Jobs, Bill Gates, and Mark Zuckerberg, started as hackers themselves. In fact, the street address of Facebook's Menlo Park, California, headquarters is 1 Hacker Way.

Hackers developed the computer technologies you use every day: the TCP/IP backbone of the modern internet, the Linux kernels of the Android systems and Red Hat servers you interact with whether or not you're aware, the GNU Public License and MIT Public License, much of the open-source code you directly or indirectly use was published under, and so on.

Hacking can develop useful new technological applications. But hacking can also be used harmfully. The general public seems to have focused on the latter connotation of the word *hacker* in lieu of its original meaning.

Many computer programmers, cybersecurity professionals, software engineers, and other computer technology specialists call themselves hackers, in the spirit of the original meaning of the word. If someone innovates with computer technology, you can safely call them a hacker.

I'm an advocate of an organization called Hacking Is Not a Crime, led by my friends Bryan McAninch, Chloé Messdaghi, and Phillip Wylie. Wylie is also the coauthor of the first book I cowrote for Wiley, *The Pentester Blueprint*. The book you're reading right now is my debut solo work for Wiley. And Wylie isn't related to Charles Wiley, who founded this company back in 1807. But perhaps this illustrates how tight knit the cybersecurity and hacker communities are: we tend to know each other quite well.

I'm an idea person within the cybersecurity community, so my contribution to Hacking Is Not a Crime's mission to promote the positive use of the word *hacker* is to use my work in the media and writing books like this in a mindful and responsible way. During the many years I have been writing about cybersecurity and hacking, I always refer to the people who use computer technology to harm as *cyberattackers*, *cybercriminals*, or *cyber threat actors*. This distinction is a vital pillar of both cybersecurity culture and hacker culture.

Even if you're 100 percent businessperson and 0 percent computer geek, understanding this will help you work with cybersecurity professionals and foster a strong security culture.

What Is Security Culture?

Lifestyle and wellness writer Tim Ferris once said, "Culture is what happens when people are left to their own devices." There are all kinds of cultures in our world, from ethnic cultures and national cultures to the goth subculture I belong to. Humanity is comprised of perhaps millions of different cultures, depending on your definition of the word. And chances are you belong to multiple cultures. As for myself, some of the cultures I belong to in addition to goth culture are hacker culture, cybersecurity culture, autistic culture, Anglo-Canadian culture, and JRPG, anime, and manga fan cultures.

If you work in business, you probably know what corporate culture is. It's how the people in your company behave, how the people in your company feel about it, and the attitudes and styles your company reinforces, whether that's done deliberately or accidentally. Corporate culture can affect employee morale, which can have a measurable effect on your bottom line.

A strong security culture encourages the people in your company to behave in ways that facilitate your resilience to cyberattacks and help protect your precious data.

I spoke to J. Wolfgang Goerlich, Duo Security advisory CISO of Cisco Systems. CISO stands for chief information security officer. CISOs bridge the gap between the suits and the nerds. Goerlich has years of experience in securing corporate business computer networks. Here's what he told me about security culture:

> Security culture comes from a partnership between security champions and security advocates. A security advocate is a member of the security team who focuses on getting practices into the hands of the workforce. It's more common for us to talk about security champions. A security champion is a member of the business itself, who collaborates with the security team on best practices. A culture of security has advocates working with champions to interpret and implement security controls. In a well-run security practice, controls will be usable and widely adopted, because of the partnership of advocates and champions.
>
> All security controls are useless if it is ignored. Good security is usable security. Good security is adopted security. The starting point, then, is empathy and kindness for the people we are charged with defending.

Daniel Chromek is CISO for ESET, a major developer of antivirus software and various security products. I believe that everyone in your organization needs to develop good security habits. Here's what Chromek told me about that:

> I would stress the word *everyone*. I'm in a better position compared to my peers (CISOs of other companies, including those outside of the cybersecurity industry) as we are a security company. This means multiple things. It's easier to explain to my business managers, as they natively understand that "we are a security company" means our brand is based on the security of the company. And even people in departments that don't need to understand security management understand that branding is important.
>
> Security culture means that part of awareness training is decentralized. If someone is targeted by phishing, then they can speak to a colleague in the same room (now virtual) and ask them to take a look into it instead of going through an IT ticketing system.
>
> People aware of security can smell if they are being deceived by FUD, so the communication from the security team needs to be straightforward. (Both Merriam-Webster and Urban Dictionary define FUD as fear, uncertainty, and doubt.) Also, security-aware people can point out bad (security) control selection or implementation very quickly by replacing auditors or specialists.
>
> Of course, the security culture is not a replacement for security controls, but it helps in all kind of controls, even unpleasant ones.

As with all the work you must do to keep your company secure, establishing and maintaining *a strong security culture isn't a project you set then forget*, as some infomercial spokespeople love to say about their As Seen on TV products. It's a constant, everyday process. It's something you build and maintain over the years. And if you neglect it, it will die. I love cybersecurity expert Bruce Schneier's ideas, so I'll quote him again as I often do in my writing:

> Security is a process, not a product.

How to Foster a Strong Security Culture

As I've mentioned, a strong security culture doesn't stop at your IT department. Every single person in your organization, from the bottom of the corporate hierarchy to the top, must be part of it.

Everyone in your company is relevant to your cybersecurity in some way or another. Your employees and contractors use your computer network, whether they're in the company workplace or working from home. Security guards and receptionists control physical access to the buildings that contain your computers. Your other employees could also mistakenly or deliberately let someone in your building who doesn't belong there, granting a possibly hostile entity physical access to your computers.

Every single thing your company's employees do with your computers, networks, and buildings can affect your security posture in a positive or negative way.

A strong security culture begins when everyone understands how they can affect your security and they are willing to be accountable for that. Next, you need to promote security awareness. As with everything security-related, security training isn't something you should do only once. People in your organization need frequent security training and reminders about proper security habits.

One of the most important things you can do is to train your workers to resist social engineering attempts. Explain what phishing is and the various ways it can manifest through phone calls, text messages, emails, web pages, and social media posts. Teach them that cyberattackers could pretend to be a person or company they trust, and to engage in healthy skepticism. And you must support that skepticism by reminding them that they won't be reprimanded for questioning if your chief executive officer (CEO) or tech support workers are who they say they are when they phone, email, or text message them.

Your email servers could have robust antivirus software that scans all email attachments that go through the system. Nonetheless, no antivirus software is perfect. Malicious email attachments are one of the most common ways that cyberattackers acquire unauthorized access to computer systems. So, part of your company's regular security training should be a reminder to only open email attachments that they expect to receive, from senders they're familiar with.

You probably detect a pattern here. Whether information is communicated over the phone or through your computer networks, your people must remember to be cautious about who they grant access to, and to what those people have access. There are lots of different lessons you must frequently teach your workers, but they're all extensions of that theme. That's what security awareness is all about, the bedrock of your security culture.

Helen Patton teaches information security at Ohio State University. She shared some security awareness training tips with me:

> Awareness training should be broader than just the company's data, with the theory that they will more likely apply security skills to stuff they care about first (family, friends) and then bring those habits to work too.
>
> Awareness training should be about building advocates, not just partners. Reward them for good security behaviors—visibly, loudly. Don't punish for bad behaviors—naming and shaming just breeds anti-security workarounds.

So, those are the ideas you must encourage your people to remember. But how can you motivate them to be engaged? Well, as much as my love of cybersecurity knowledge drives my career, money is one of my main motivations. I have no interest in becoming super wealthy, but I need money to pay my bills and buy food, video games, and Demonia boots. I'm not unusual, except perhaps in my taste for footwear. People do well in their jobs because they want and need money, a necessity in our market economy. Security Journey CEO Chris Romeo also sees money as a useful motivator to get your employees to do good things for cybersecurity:

> When someone goes through the mandatory security awareness program and completes it successfully, give them a high-five or something more substantial. A simple cash reward of $100 is a huge motivator for people and will cause them to remember the security lesson that provided the money.

I discuss how to build a security team in step 2. But yeah, dangle a monetary carrot in front of your workers! It won't hurt to give that a try. And as Romeo implies, $100 is much cheaper than a data breach!

Here's some more advice for fostering a strong security culture: make security awareness and training fun. In my writing, I convey my emotional and enthusiastic personality. I also get silly sometimes. I know that by writing that way, I can retain your interest and attention more effectively than if my writing was dry and boring, like in a lot of technical documentation and textbooks. If you find security concepts to be exciting and fascinating, you can express that attitude in how you conduct your security training and reminders.

It may help to quiz your employees about security in the style of a game show. Maybe you can search Randall Munroe's archive of xkcd web comics and find the perfect comic strip to complement a security concept you're teaching.

Be creative with how you present security knowledge and encourage good habits in a fun way. If you feel that your imagination is lacking, there's probably a creative thinker in your company who can help you with this.

Train your workers regularly, and give them frequent reminders of how they can work and interact with your computer systems in a more secure way. Now you're well on your way to fostering a strong security culture. But before we move onto step 2, there's one more thing I'd like you to keep in mind.

Security Leaders on Security Culture

Security leaders believe strongly in the importance of security culture. I asked some of these leaders for their thoughts on how an organization can improve their security culture. Their ideas were varied, but they all included improving relationships. For example, Andrew Gish-Johnson at Carnegie Mellon University stressed visibility and a willingness to help. He said, "Figuring out how to do things right is tough. Finding people to help is tough. If the organization doesn't know who to talk to or finds you're not helpful, they're avoiding you as much as possible." But if, as the CISO, you can make sure the rest of the company knows who you are and what your role is, you can help improve your security culture.

Nav Bassi, the CISO at the University of Victoria, stressed "awareness and education," while my friend Larry, a good cybersecurity leader but a very private man, said that "gamification (making educational material like a video game)" can help ensure employees understand cybersecurity well enough that they can maintain the security culture.

What Makes a Good CISO?

Not all organizations have chief information security officers. For the most part, they're like chief technical officers, but they're focused on cybersecurity. The nature of this executive role bridges the gap between nontechnical business leaders ("the suits") and the IT department ("the nerds").

Sometimes a company will outsource functions of the CISO role to a managed service provider or some other sort of third party. Either way, if your organization has a CISO, they're the top of the cybersecurity hierarchy. A CISO's job is to lead an organization's security team and to work with other executives to make sure the organization meets its cybersecurity goals. If a company gets hit by a major cyberattack that costs them millions of dollars, their CISO will be very stressed out.

I asked some security leaders what makes an effective CISO. In a nutshell, CISOs need to be able to work well with people. It helps to understand cybersecurity and information technology in general. But people skills are paramount in the CISO role. You need to be able to explain to other executives, such as the chief financial officer, why money should be allocated for a security budget. You need to be able to explain why spending $500,000 on cybersecurity can save the company $5 million. Further, you must also be able to lead your security team, including the people in your IT department.

Andreas Bogk, a principal security architect, also believes the CISO needs to be able to remain calm in a crisis. Nav Bassi thinks curiosity and resilience are important traits in a CISO. Randy Marchany, the CISO at Virginia Tech, believes in a strong team and thinks the CISO needs to be able to trust, defend, and cultivate the growth of the team. These characteristics all demonstrate the need for a CISO to be able to work well with other people.

The Biggest Mistakes Businesses Make When It Comes to Cybersecurity

I asked business cybersecurity leaders about the biggest mistakes organizations make when it comes to cybersecurity. Their answers included trying to solve a problem by buying off-the-shelf software, keeping investment in cybersecurity to a minimum, and believing that having employees who are compliant means that the company is secure. Mitch Parker, the CISO of Indiana University Health, put together his "top 11" mistakes:

- Assuming that IT costs are sunk costs and that IT is capable of handling all issues with minimal effort or intervention.
- Not doing or ignoring a risk assessment.
- Not addressing or developing a risk management plan.
- Not developing good internal processes to assess and address risks.
- Under-resourcing information security initiatives either through lack of funding, team members, or both.
- Assuming that cyber insurance is an appropriate risk transference mechanism. As of 2021, when this was written, the major cyber insurance carriers are becoming more stringent with who they insure. They are denying higher-risk customers policies due to ransomware payouts causing significant financial losses.
- Leadership allowing their teams to bypass security controls and identified risks to facilitate the business, even if there is a high probability of a breach.
- Assuming that security events will never happen to them for any number of imagined reasons.
- Cutting security and IT costs out of projects to increase profitability on return-on-investment calculations.
- Leadership not supporting security and information risk management as a required business function.
- Overreliance on tools or services to address security needs based on inflated expectations and little analysis.

Even if you aren't a CISO, these are valuable tips for when you design your company's cybersecurity program. It's always best to learn from others the easy way, rather than learn the hard way by making the same mistakes yourself.

The Psychological Phases of a Cybersecurity Professional

You will probably work with cybersecurity professionals at some point or another. I want to help you to foster a strong security culture by teaching you what I've learned about how we think. Understanding this will be a big help in security hardening your organization.

When people start learning cybersecurity, they often believe that computer software, hardware, and networks can be made 100 percent secure. That's the first phase. "I must learn about everything that makes computers vulnerable, so those things can be completely remedied, and then there'll be no more security problems!" But as the first months and years of their studies progress, they learn that absolutely nothing can be made 100 percent secure.

The first problem is the complexity of computer systems. I love video games, so I'll use them as an example. Video games on Nintendo Entertainment System (NES) cartridges typically ranged from 128 to 384 kilobytes in size, with a few games, such as Kirby's Adventure, coming in at a relatively whopping 768 kilobytes. All of that code was written in assembly language, the code computers send directly to the CPU. NES games could have a few bugs here and there, but they couldn't have a lot of bugs and remain functional, because the games were programmed in a simpler way. Plus, the fewer lines of code a program has, the fewer bugs it can have and still run. Any programmer can tell you that.

As of this writing, most of the games I play these days are on my PS4 and Nintendo Switch, eighth-generation video game consoles. It's impossible to make these more technologically complex games in pure assembly language. Their developers use multiple computer programming languages, large media assets such as polygonal environments, sound and video files, and sophisticated game engines such as Unreal Engine 4 and Rockstar Advanced Game Engine. Eighth-generation games are often 20 gigabytes in size, frequently over 50 gigabytes. That's a lot more code than an NES game, and today's internet-connected video game consoles are constantly installing multiple gigabyte patches. The first stable version of a game is never the last.

Debugging today's complex video games is much harder work. And the best developers know that even well-designed and maintained games will have at least hundreds of bugs. Their complexity causes this challenge.

The greater complexity of today's AAA video games is parallel to the complexity of today's corporate computer networks. The software, hardware, and design of networks are all much more complicated than they were in the 1980s and '90s. Many companies have hybrid networks where some of their servers may be on their premises while their other servers are provided by a cloud service such as Amazon Web Service (AWS). The internet interfaces with their networks at many points as a functional necessity, but the internet is the source of most cyber threats. Combine all that with trying to get your users and employees to behave in secure ways, and you'll understand that complexity is one of the main reasons why nothing is 100 percent secure.

Then there's the compromise to be made between security and usability. The most secure computers in the world are airgapped, meaning that they are locked down as much as technically possible. They're usually not connected to the internet, or often to any network at all. Their USB ports are disabled. The people using them have to go through layers of physical security, such as locked doors with fingerprint scanners. All of those security measures make airgapped computers difficult to use. That's why they're usually deployed only when they access data that's considered highly sensitive.

It would be a big problem if most or all of the computers in your network were airgapped. Most of the facets of your computer network must be usable. But you also don't want your computers to be too accessible. So, you'll need to find the right compromise between security and usability. When you, as a cybersecurity professional, learn that some risks must be accepted for practical reasons, that reinforces the lesson that nothing can be made 100 percent secure and helps you remain vigilant. If you think any computer system can be completely secure, you may forget that security is a constant process, which can result in any number of things going wrong. Understanding that security risks and vulnerabilities will always exist will improve the quality of your work.

Understanding that nothing is completely secure often leads to the next phase, overconfidence. *Some of the most well-known cybersecurity professionals are still at this phase and may never evolve from it.* These cybersecurity professionals often think, "Why are my users so foolish? They do all these foolish things. How can they be so ignorant? My silly users are the security problem! As for me, I'm a cybersecurity expert. So, my habits are perfect, and I could never fall for a social engineering attack. I'm too smart for that!" Admittedly, I didn't evolve past this phase until a few years ago. Here are the problems with this kind of thinking.

First, you're not going to improve security by treating users and employees like they're foolish fools who are beneath your wisdom. As important as it is to teach people to develop better security habits, well-designed computer security accepts the realities of human nature.

For example, the January 2021 attack on the US Capitol building happened a few weeks prior to this writing. Thousands of right-wing extremists, some of whom worked in law enforcement, tried to seize the US Capitol building because they believed that Joe Biden won the 2020 election illegitimately. They believed Donald Trump was cheated out of a re-election they thought he deserved. Most of the attackers were armed and dangerous. When security professionals with access to the Capitol's computer system became aware of the attack, they sent an evacuation warning to the computer screens of many Capitol building employees and workers: something to the effect of "Get out now. This building is in danger!"

One of the insurgents took a photo of a computer screen with an evacuation warning and posted it to social media. I saw it on

Twitter. Not only could the warning be seen, but sensitive information in a worker's email application was also visible.

A prominent person in our industry criticized the Capitol building worker for being foolish enough to leave that sensitive data on their computer screen as they fled to safety. Other more sensible and empathetic members of the cybersecurity community replied that the worker likely was afraid that they could be killed and their life is the most important thing to protect. If I were that Capitol worker, I also wouldn't have shut down my computer before running away. Would you? Probably not. Seconds could mean life or death in an active shooter incident.

The computer system could have been designed in such a way that evacuation warnings could trigger the computers to automatically shut down or otherwise suspend the user's session. The computer system could have protected the sensitive data on those screens without the need for user interaction so workers could focus on their physical safety.

If you look down at your users, your attitude will be detrimental to fostering a strong security culture. A false sense of superiority is problematic in other ways too. Even cybersecurity professionals have bad habits. Until I started using password managers a few years ago, I used the same password for multiple online services. The problem with doing that is if one of my passwords is breached, cyberattackers could engage in credential stuffing—trying the same password with my other accounts. People reuse passwords frequently, so credential stuffing attacks are often effective. I tackled my password reuse problem, but I likely have some other bad security habits too. If I overestimate my own security, I won't be sufficiently vigilant.

About a year ago, I also learned that cybersecurity professionals are becoming more frequent phishing targets in advanced persistent threat cyberattacks. We also tend to overestimate our inability to be fooled by social engineering, to our detriment.

Cybersecurity professionals must learn humility, for our users and for ourselves, and that's an important thing to keep in mind in order to foster a strong security culture.

Chapter 2
Step 2: Build a Security Team

Congratulations! You've reached the most important chapter of this book. It's also probably the most controversial chapter of this book. Every single word I've written in this book has been carefully chosen; every word has purpose and value. I recommend that you read the entire book at your own pace. You likely paid for the entirety of this book, and you should get as much out of it as you can, but if you can read only one chapter of this book, make sure it's this one. Let me tell you why.

If hiring the right cybersecurity professionals is the one thing you do right, then you will have people in place to help with the other seven steps in this book. If you've forgotten the other seven steps, doing this one step well will make up for it. All eight steps are vital for properly preparing your organization for the evolving cyber threat landscape, but this step is the one you'll have the least amount of support with outside of this book.

In the cybersecurity industry, there is a lot of bad advice about hiring, but there's a lot of good advice too. Finding the right sources of good advice is a similar concept to hiring the right people. If you're starting your security program from square one, how are you going to determine who you should be listening to? This chapter is all about how to choose the right people.

With that in mind, please think critically about my advice too. If my ideas can't withstand scrutiny, then they're not worth the paper (or eBook data) they're written on.

Why Step 2 Is Controversial

So, you're probably wondering why I think this chapter is the most controversial in this whole book. It's because I'm going to address what I and many other people in our industry consider to be a common and harmful myth—the cybersecurity skills gap.

Here's the common definition of the cybersecurity skills gap:

> There's a wide variety of cybersecurity roles. They require specific and highly technical skills. Colleges and universities (and possibly third-party certification bodies as well) aren't producing enough graduates with the specific and highly technical skills that are needed for the wide variety of cybersecurity roles. That's why companies struggle to hire the right cybersecurity professionals. Cybersecurity has a supply chain problem, and possibly a job applicant problem too.

I wrote that definition from memory, being careful to be objective and avoid constructing a straw man fallacy regarding what believers in the cybersecurity skills gap actually think. To be extra sure I didn't craft a straw man, I tried to find a definition on the web. The phrase *cybersecurity skills gap* returns many pages worth of search results. I looked at a few resources written by people and entities that believe in the gap. But they all seem to assume you already know what the phrase means, and they believe that the meaning of and existence of the cybersecurity skills gap are givens.

Some of the entities that believe in the cybersecurity skills gap include the Enterprise Strategy Group (ESG), an IT service management company, and the Information Systems Security Association (ISSA), whose members typically work in the corporate side of cybersecurity. These two organizations collaborated on a report entitled "The Life and Times of Cybersecurity Professionals 2020" (`https://www.issa.org/wp-content/uploads/2020/07/ESG-ISSA-Research-Report-Cybersecurity-Professionals-Jul-2020.pdf`), where they addressed the skills gap.

> This year, 70% of ISSA members believe their organization has been impacted by the global cybersecurity skills shortage. ESG/ISSA added a question to this year's survey to answer this question. The results are distressing—45% believe the cybersecurity skills shortage (and its impact) have gotten worse over the past few years.

Based on this discussion, most ISSA members believe there's a skills gap, or "skills shortage." Although they do not define the gap explicitly, they address the impact and suggest some solutions.

The other entity that's known for endorsing the idea of a cybersecurity skills gap is Cybersecurity Ventures (`https://cybersecurityventures.com/jobs/`), a research and publishing company in the cybersecurity industry. Here's what Steve Morgan, its editor-in-chief, has to say:

> The *New York Times* reports that a stunning statistic is reverberating in cybersecurity: Cybersecurity Ventures' prediction that there will be 3.5 million unfilled cybersecurity jobs globally by 2021, up from one million positions in 2014.

I think ISSA members and Steve Morgan are correct that there are nowhere near as many people employed in cybersecurity roles as there should be. A lack of people working in areas such as incident response, digital forensics, penetration testing, secure application development, security operations centers, managed service providers, and so on is making companies of all sizes and in all industries a lot more vulnerable to cyberattack than they otherwise would be. There are lot of effective automated tools that can help organizations improve their security posture a great deal if they're configured and implemented properly, but human beings cannot be replaced by automation; they can only be augmented by it. As I'm writing this in early 2021, I am predicting that in 2050 and beyond, we will still need some humans in cybersecurity roles.

Although some of us in the cybersecurity industry agree that we need more people in cybersecurity roles, we argue that the "cybersecurity skills gap" is a harmful myth. We believe that the wrong party is being blamed. Those who believe in the gap tend to blame the group of people with the least amount of power in this equation: students and job applicants of all ages. Skills gap believers assume something is lacking in the people who apply for cybersecurity jobs. Believers may place some of the fault with the institutions that exist to train people. But the people who graduate from or become certified by these institutions are being blamed as well.

I find this practice to be unethical. I believe that blaming the people with the least amount of power is uncaring and impractical. The organizations that hire people have the most amount of power. They often have millions or even billions of dollars of capital. With all that wealth comes an awful lot of influence. When people run for political office, they find that having more campaign money means it's easier to get their message out to voters, and therefore they're more likely to get elected. The same applies to private companies and advertising budgets. Advertising costs money, and money is power.

A few students and job applicants come from wealthy families, and they can spend as much money on school tuition and certification exams as they'd like. If it takes them a few years or more to get employed, that's okay. Because they don't really need the money, they don't worry about how they're going to pay their bills, and cybersecurity is simply a passion for them.

Those few wealthy people are the minority. The majority of people find college or university education prohibitively expensive in countries like the United States, Canada, and the United Kingdom, where the government doesn't cover the expense of higher education. Some may be lucky enough to earn full scholarships, but the majority of people in those countries have to take burdensome student loans or otherwise pay upfront. Tuition and books can cost $10,000 or more per year. Plus, time spent in school is time that can't be spent generating the income those students need for housing, food, and other living expenses. Far too many students have to compromise the quality of their education because they have to work 20 hours or more per week for survival money. The last time I walked through a college campus here in Toronto, I was tremendously saddened to see a food bank for students. I have a feeling that hundreds of other campuses in Canada, the United States, and the United Kingdom also have food banks. This is a dark reality, indeed.

And whether or not a graduate can find employment in their field, people are often in debt from their student loans into middle age and beyond. According to the Consumer Financial Protection Bureau's "Snapshot of Older Consumers and Student Loan Debt" from January 2017 (`https://files.consumerfinance.gov/f/documents/201701_cfpb_OA-Student-Loan-Snapshot.pdf`):

> The number of consumers age 60 and older with student loan debt has quadrupled over the last decade in the United States, and the average amount they owe has also dramatically increased. In 2015, older consumers owed an estimated $66.7 billion in student loans.

Although the report is four years old as of this writing, my educated assumption is the situation hasn't improved since then.

Now, you may be thinking that students and job applicants who are smothered in decades of debt and sometimes struggling to buy food aren't to blame for the cybersecurity skills gap. But some people are bringing up understandable concerns that schools aren't teaching people the right knowledge and skills. So, it's fair to blame the institutions instead, right?

Colleges and universities may deserve some of the blame. I'm sure some computer science and information technology programs are better than others (depending on your criteria), and the quality and industry relevance of an education program likely varies from school to school and instructor to instructor.

There are also organizations such as CompTIA, EC-Council, and (ISC)² that offer cybersecurity industry certifications that can be obtained both within and outside of college and university programs. These certifications are designed to demonstrate to employers that an applicant has some specific knowledge and skills for particular cybersecurity roles, and for information technology roles in general. Sometimes people spend thousands of dollars on certification guides and exams so they can acquire employment credentials without the need for college or university.

Perhaps one of the reasons why organizations like CompTIA, EC-Council, and $(ISC)^2$ exist in the first place is because college and university degrees aren't useful training for cybersecurity roles on their own. So, certifications are needed to augment or substitute for traditional college degrees. This was likely more of a problem in the 1990s and 2000s when many new cybersecurity roles had to be invented to manage new technologies. School curriculums likely couldn't keep up with the rapidly evolving pace of technological change. (Schools may now be better at keeping pace.) Big tech companies such as Microsoft and Cisco also have their own certifications that demonstrate knowledge and skills with their particular products and services.

But like college and university tuition, studying for industry certifications can be expensive. And it can cost hundreds or thousands of dollars to write an exam. If you don't pass your exam the first time, there's usually no refund. The best you can do is study more or study differently and pay to take the exam again. Students who might struggle affording tuition and books may also struggle to afford acquiring certifications.

If governments assumed the full expense of tuition and study programs as they do in some European countries, obviously it would be much easier for nonwealthy people to obtain the credentials that they need to get employed in well-paying cyber jobs. That may address some of the supposed "skills gap" problem.

But there's another problem that employers often overlook, often because acknowledging the problem makes them look bad. Employers are largely to blame for the lack of qualified applicants for cybersecurity positions. They're the party with the most money, influence, and power.

Far too many people in my industry have seen job listings that look something like the following:

Security Operations Center (SOC) Specialists, Entry Level

Reports to the SOC manager. Must have:

- 10 years of Kubernetes (open-source container orchestration system) experience
- 5 years of Windows Server 2019 experience
- 5 years of Red Hat Enterprise Linux 8 experience
- A master's degree in computer science or better
- Demonstrable familiarity with the AT&T Cybersecurity AlienVault Unified Security Management (SIEM) platform
- (ISC)^2 CISSP (Certified Information Systems Security Professional)
- EC-Council CEH (Certified Ethical Hacker)
- PMI PMP (Project Management Professional)
- Contributed to at least one entry in the CVE (Common Vulnerabilities and Exposures database)
- Metasploit Framework experience
- Compensation range: $40,000–$50,000 per year, based on experience
- Looking to hire by August 2021

Let's pick apart how horrifying a job posting like that is and what's wrong with it.

- The (fictional) job posting is from 2021, but Kubernetes wasn't initially released until June 2014. Kubernetes' own developers don't even have 10 years of Kubernetes experience yet. And why should someone outside of DevOps or related areas have containerization expertise?
- Windows Server 2019 wasn't released until October 2018. Demanding five years of experience by 2021 is also an impossible expectation without a time machine.

- The beta version of Red Hat Enterprise Linux 8 wasn't released until November 2018, and the stable version wasn't released until May 2019.
- A master's degree in computer science requires three or four years of undergraduate school and another two or three years of graduate school. The combined tuition for that is likely $50,000 to $100,000, depending on the school and many other factors. This company is requiring all of that for an entry-level position?
- People usually don't become familiar with AT&T Cybersecurity AlienVault Unified Security Management or any other SIEM platform until they've already worked in a security operations center.
- Way too many employers demand a CISSP. The CISSP is as close to a PhD as cybersecurity certifications get. You can't even obtain the certification unless you already have, according to (ISC)², "a minimum of five years of direct full-time security work experience in two or more of the (ISC)² information security domains (CBK)." Only roles at the very top of the cybersecurity hierarchy, such as chief information security officers (CISOs), should ask for a CISSP in the first place. Unfortunately, too many employers want applicants to have a CISSP before they're employed for the first time. How could entry-level applicants already have five years or more of specific industry experience?
- The CEH is for demonstrating penetration testing knowledge. Penetration testing is an offensive security task. The SOC is a defensive security role.
- Why should SOC analysts have project management certifications?
- To be able to contribute to the CVE database, you need to find a zero-day vulnerability, a vulnerability security that researchers haven't discovered before. Bug hunters and penetration testers find new vulnerabilities. Again, this is an offensive security matter. In defensive security roles, you're supposed to patch, mitigate, or otherwise be aware of vulnerabilities, not discover them.

- Metasploit Framework is a network vulnerability scanning platform, often used in penetration testing. Again, SOC analysts don't do penetration testing.
- Let me get this straight. The employer wants to pay a maximum of $50,000 for perhaps $100,000 worth of formal education, plus five years or more industry experience (what a CISSP requires), an impossible amount of experience with certain applications and technologies, and a bunch of skills SOC analysts don't need in the first place—plus SIEM experience that people are unlikely to have until they've already worked in a SOC? The employer not only wants to underpay for all of that experience and knowledge, but they also demand impossible skills and knowledge.

You may think I've constructed a straw man in this fictional job posting. But many people in my industry have seen job postings with the same problems: "entry-level" positions requiring CISSPs and master's degrees, more experience with applications than the time the applications have even existed, and skills and experience in areas that aren't relevant to the role in the first place. "Entry level" in these situations means the employers want to pay you like you're new, but you must have 20 years of industry experience or an impossible combination of skills. Those same companies whine about the "cybersecurity skills gap," and they blame schools and certification bodies and the job applicants themselves.

Those positions in those companies stay unfilled, and a lack of security staff makes those organizations a lot more vulnerable to cyberattacks and cyber incidents. They lose millions of dollars in those incidents while they keep blaming the party with the least amount of power.

So, don't be like those companies. Take a better approach. This chapter contains my advice for hiring the right people. It's time for positive thinking.

For further reading, I recommend checking out the articles on the mythical "cybersecurity skills gap" that my friend, security evangelist Alyssa Miller, has written on her blog: `https://alyssasec.com/tag/skills-gap`.

How to Hire the Right Security Team. . .the Right Way

First, you should be open-minded about job applicants. It's realistic to expect a CISSP for a CISO role that pays $200,000 per year, and you can expect a CEH, an Offensive Security Certified Professional (OSCP), or a CompTIA PenTest+ from a relatively inexperienced penetration tester. Expecting CompTIA A+, Network+, and Security+ for most junior cybersecurity roles is fine. But it may not be a good idea to consider certifications to be an absolute requirement, especially if a relatively junior job has been vacant for a month or more.

Wiley's own Sybex imprint and other publishers make excellent guides for studying for specific certifications. In *The Pentester Blueprint*, which I cowrote with Phillip Wylie, we recommend that people who want a career as a pentester (short for penetration tester) pursue the CEH, OSCP, and other certifications. The same applies to cybersecurity roles in general. You should research which certifications are relevant to the areas of cybersecurity you're interested in and try your best to acquire those certifications on your own. It'll definitely help when you're looking for a job.

But wouldn't it be lovely if more employers bought those books for their employees and contractors, paid them while they're studying and writing exams, and invested in their training completely? The effort needs to come from the security professional, but the expense can be covered by the employer. Whatever it costs an employer to buy books and training videos and to manage lower productivity from the worker while they're studying, it's still much less expensive than seeing cybersecurity roles stay vacant and not having enough staff when costly cyber incidents hit. Those incidents will happen; they're inevitable.

Sometimes employers are afraid that if they spend a lot of time and money on training, employees will take those new skills, leave the company, and use those skills with their competitor. However, employees are much more likely to work hard and be loyal to employers that invest in them and pay them well. Internal training is especially important when jobs require niche skills and knowledge. Some of my colleagues in the industry have been rejected for jobs because they have experience with a year-old version of an application, but not with the version that was released a few months ago. It's infuriating.

Too many employers expect employees to be completely ready for jobs with niche skills right out of the box, no training required. And I suspect sometimes that they push the "cybersecurity skills gap" myth because they want the burden of training to be on the schools and employees, but not on the companies themselves. This is a problem with dreadful consequences.

Some of my friends are developers. They've told me of the dreaded whiteboard interview. Big tech companies, especially in Silicon Valley and Washington State, expect developer job applicants to solve mathematically intense problems with particular programming code, in marker and on the whiteboard, on the spot, with no help. In truth, even the best developers are constantly looking up how to code or debug certain things on the web. In a programmer's actual job, they can always look stuff up. So, why expect developers to solve problems without any help in the job interview process?

Security Team Tips from Security Leaders

I asked security leaders for their advice when hiring a security team. Several of the leaders stressed the importance of having a diverse team—relating to their background as well as their experience. Randy Marchany believes "Each individual will have a different set of life experiences and may see risk differently. A diverse workforce will ensure you are looking at security from various angles and will challenge your org to not just approach security from a status quo view."

Other leaders mentioned how valuable the junior employees are. According to Andreas Bogk, "Junior people are often very motivated, eager to learn, and bring in a fresh perspective." Nav Bassi said, "I am a firm believer in growing from within, meaning recruiting for junior positions and developing junior positions into senior positions by investing in professional development and participation in new projects and initiatives." In discussing the skills gap myth, J. Wolfgang Goerlich also addressed junior employees: "We need better skills in developing entry-level talent into mid-level professionals, and in promoting mid-level professionals into senior positions."

Another area the leaders discussed was educational and work experience. Bogk said, "Certifications are en vogue, and nice to have, but I value curiosity and a desire to learn over a piece of paper." Marchany likes to think outside the box: "Don't focus on traditional methods that only look at degreed and cyber or infosec skilled individuals. Seek out the problem solvers, detail-oriented and the creative thinkers no matter what their existing job role or experience is. Seek out the artists, musicians, accountants, auditors, programmers, or help desk professionals."

Additionally, it is important to invest in the cybersecurity team, expanding it as the company grows. You must also ensure that the team has the infrastructure they need to do their job effectively.

The "Culture Fit"—Yuck!

Here's another huge problem in the hiring process. Employers call it "culture fit." No matter how much human resources managers and other people who make hiring decisions may tell themselves otherwise, the hiring process is never completely objective. People make messy, emotional decisions in the hiring process. We're only human; we can't help it. The only way to manage subjectivity is to acknowledge that it exists in the first place. I know I'm a highly emotional thinker, even in some of my most technical writing. In fact, I think my emotional style of writing has been an asset in my career. Surely you're having fun reading this book? I talk to you like I'm having an animated conversation with you. My personality just drips off of every page.

But emotional thinking can be harmful when we deny that we do it. People want to hire people who remind them of themselves, even if they're only subconsciously aware of that thinking. Herein lies the "culture fit" problem. Employers use that phrase to rationalize only hiring people they personally like.

The result of making hiring decisions partly based on "culture fit" is disastrous to organizations. People with power and influence in companies are often from privileged groups such as white, male, cisgender, heterosexual, nondisabled people with generic names like Jason Smith (that's my romantic partner's name actually—no offense, darling) from middle class or wealthy backgrounds and from Ivy League schools who know the "right" people.

Some of the harm is done by denying people high-paying tech jobs if they come from different racial or ethnic backgrounds or are gay, transgender, fat, short, disabled, or from other marginalized groups.

But limiting the pool of people you hire from is harmful to organizations in direct ways. Broaden your scope, and give people who are different from you and other people in your company a chance to shine. For example, the national teams that compete in the World Cup (soccer, or football outside of the United States and Canada) consist of people who are primarily from the nation they're representing, in contrast to NHL hockey teams or NBA basketball teams, with players who are seldom from their home cities. My mother's side of the family is from Malta, and although the Maltese are very passionate about the sport they (we?) call football, the country never ranks high in international competitions. Countries with much larger populations such as Brazil, England, Italy, and Germany tend to do much better in the competition. English people aren't inherently better at soccer than Maltese people. Rather, the larger countries have a much larger talent pool to choose from. The same situation applies to finding the best security professionals. You'll find better security professionals when you consider a broader range of applicants, rather than looking for a "culture fit."

I haven't talked about myself enough yet, and this is my book, so let me talk about myself some more. I may be just the kind of person who gets excluded when employers look for a "culture fit." I'm female, and 25 percent or less of people in tech jobs are my gender.

But I'm also disabled. I don't necessarily "look" disabled, but I'm autistic, and I have ADHD. As I'm writing this book, I'm constantly stimming at my desk with an earbud cord and other stim toys. Thank goodness my career has reached a point where people in this industry know who I am. But when I used to go to job interviews, I had to practice every bit of self-control that I have to "mask" my autistic traits. I worked hard to keep my hands still and in my lap, make eye contact, but not too much eye contact, and keep smiling, but make my smile look natural. For a neurodivergent person like myself, that's a lot of hard work. I can manage to suppress myself for an hour or two while being interviewed, but after the interview I'm mentally exhausted and I need to recuperate at home.

In spite of this, I have low support needs. For other autistic people, masking for that long can be much more difficult, if not impossible. Either way, masking isn't good for our health. I've spoken with a lot of the most brilliant people in the cybersecurity field, and large numbers of us are autistic, ADHD, or neurodivergent in other ways. There are even a few well-known people in our industry who have confided to me that they're autistic, but they've sworn me to secrecy. And I will keep their secrets. A lot of the most brilliant technical minds are autistic, starting with Alan Turing, the father of computer science.

Many disabled people have found that companies would not hire them if their disabilities meant they can only work remotely. However, many cybersecurity and other IT jobs can be done remotely, through secured networking technologies such as SSH. The Covid-19 pandemic has forced a lot of companies to let their staff work remotely, even if they're not disabled. A lot of disabled people are justifiably angry about this. Companies should make an effort to accommodate disabled people.

The access needs disabled people have can vary greatly from person to person. Ask your disabled worker directly how your workplace can be more accessible for them. That could mean letting your staff take longer breaks or work from home, or there may be other things you can do to accommodate them. Even disabled adults often find that we aren't considered the experts on our own disabilities. This can sometimes have dangerous consequences. Besides, you could be missing out on some great cybersecurity professionals when you decide to not accommodate disabled people. Ask your disabled talent what they need in order to thrive in your company.

In addition to being neurodivergent, I have a face full of piercings, I'm goth, and I have a lot of tattoos. However, my appearance has absolutely no effect on how appropriate I am for a particular job or how well I do my job. As long as a prospective employee does not have any visible tattoos that have offensive symbols, tattoos shouldn't be an issue.

But even though my tattoos and piercings make me look "different," I'm white, cisgender, and of average height and weight for a cisgender woman. People of different races and ethnicities, transgender people, visibly disabled people, or people marginalized in other ways could face even greater hurdles to gainful employment. Cast a wide net in your hiring processes, and let diversity be your organization's strength.

Here's one final note about the "culture fit" problem. There are some cybersecurity professionals with decades of experience, but they still find they can't get hired. This is often the result of ageism. Some companies refuse to hire people in their 50s or older, whether they admit it or not. They assume that people in their 20s are better tech workers. But you're missing out on the experience of older people. Another problem is when older people have experience with applications that are five years old, but they don't have experience with the latest versions of programming languages, IDEs, firewalls, or applications.

Ideally, your security staff should come from a broad range of age groups. Your older staff members can mentor your younger staff members. If older people, or anyone else, lack the latest versions of certifications or anything else, your company can train them in the latest versions. Your organization should thrive in the long term, over years or even decades. Hire people from their 20s to their 60s right now. And as your older staff retires, your younger staff will also become older. And then they can help guide the kids who are fresh out of school. Hiring from different age groups is an asset to any company. You can benefit from the experience of older people and the fresh thinking of younger people.

Cybersecurity Budgets

The money your organization spends on cybersecurity is your cybersecurity budget. Your budget can vary greatly according to the following factors:

- The size of your organization. Obviously, a small business of 20 people will have a much smaller security budget than a large corporation of 50,000 people.
- Quantity and sensitivity of data. Healthcare and financial services typically have larger security budgets than public schools and food service due to the quantity and sensitivity of their data.
- Regulatory compliance with industry-specific regulations. Certain data security regulations pertain to particular industries. Most countries have data security legislation specific to healthcare and financial services. Complying with these regulations in addition to general data security regulations will increase the expense of your security.
- History and experience with cyberattacks. If your organization has lost millions of dollars in previous cyber incidents, such as data breaches or ransomware, recovering from those incidents and improving your company's reputation will add to your security expenses.

Before you hire a security team, you will need to determine your cybersecurity budget. The labor compensation and benefits for your team members are a major component of your security budget. Also, you may need the help of your security team leaders to determine your overall security budget. They may help you determine how much money should be spent in which areas and how it should be spent.

Depending on the needs of your organization and your industry, your cybersecurity budget could range from $10,000 per year to $100 million per year or more. That's a pretty wide range.

If you don't know where to start when it comes to determining your cybersecurity budget, here's a helpful tip I've learned from industry leaders: Consider your overall information technology budget. That's all the money your organization spends on computers, networking, all computer-related services, and IT staff. A typical cybersecurity budget is 3 to 5 percent of the overall IT budget. But if your organization is in a data-sensitive and regulatory-intensive industry such as financial services or healthcare, your cybersecurity budget may need to be 10 to 15 percent of your overall IT budget.

Design Your Perfect Security Team

You've determined your cybersecurity budget—or at least you have some vague idea of what it should be. Now you should be ready to hire a security team based on that budget. Here's my advice to get you started.

If your organization is small, with 200 employees or fewer, you may have only one or two IT workers. These people are your security team, even if security is only a part of what they do. You may need to hire a managed services provider as a third-party contractor and periodically hire third-party security testers. Your one or two IT staff should be prepared to collaborate with your contracted services. And your one or two IT people should be everyday generalists. They're network administrators and technical support, and they should be able to manage your network and endpoints in a security-minded way. For instance, your network administrator should understand how to assign privileges to user accounts and configure firewalls properly.

If your organization is medium sized, about 200 to 1,000 employees, you can afford to have a few people in dedicated cybersecurity roles. Your network administrators and technical support should be augmented by a couple of network security specialists. Your network security specialists may have certifications such as a Cisco Certified Network Associate, a CompTIA Security+, and a CompTIA Cyber Security Analyst. If you have job applicants who demonstrate an understanding of network security without certifications, consider allocating a few thousand dollars of your security budget to helping them train for and acquire these certifications. If you're a retailer or food service organization, you may need to have one staff member dedicated to securing your point-of-sale system. Your entire IT department, a legal specialist, and a PR specialist will comprise your organization's incident response team. Those are your people who deal with cyber incidents and their aftermath. Your IT staff need to act quickly as soon as indications of a cyber incident are detected, whereas your legal specialist handles the legalities, and your PR specialist decides how to inform your customers and the public of the incident as needed. Hiring a managed services provider and periodical third-party security testing is also a wise idea.

If your organization is large, more than 1,000 employees, you will need all the staff a medium-sized organization requires, with more people in each role. A large organization can support a dedicated blue team and red team. Your blue team would be defensive security specialists in areas such as incident response, digital forensics, and patch management. Your red team imitates cyberattackers by performing penetration tests and other kinds of security testing, as offensive security specialists. The vulnerabilities your red team discovers should be addressed by your blue team.

If your organization has more than 10,000 employees, you may be able to support a security operations center. This is a dedicated team that constantly watches your network logs for indications of cyber incidents through a security information and event management platform, and they also respond to other people in your organization when they suspect cyber incidents. This is another defensive security role.

My best advice if you're unsure of how to proceed in hiring your security team is to ask people in the online cybersecurity community for advice. Although we don't work free of charge, we will often gladly give you free advice if you ask us specific questions.

Twitter and LinkedIn are some of the best places to find us. Search for *#infosec* and *#cybersecurity*. You should also check out Marcus J. Carey and Jennifer Jin's Tribe of Hackers book series to find industry experts who can give you tips for hiring a security team that are specific to your needs. In addition to the first book in the series, there's also *Tribe of Hackers Red Team*, *Tribe of Hackers Blue Team*, and *Tribe of Hackers Security Leaders*. For the sake of full disclosure, I'm included in the first book, and many of my friends are featured in the series. You'll soon find the cybersecurity industry is a small and well-connected world.

Chapter 3
Step 3: Regulatory Compliance

Even if you've never worked in cybersecurity, you've probably noticed that every so often, a huge data breach incident makes mainstream news. Data breaches happen every day, whether we know about them or not. One of the most disturbing things I learned in my years of reporting cyber incidents in the media is that the breaches we're aware of are only the tip of the iceberg. Many breaches lie undiscovered, like the underwater portion of an iceberg.

There is no data to back this up, but I have heard anecdotes. My experience in the industry has taught me that for every big data breach story in the news, there are at least 20 that companies know about but are keeping to themselves and 100 that not even their targets know about. I will examine some actual data breach research later.

Step 3 focuses on regulatory compliance. The regulatory compliance your business should be concerned about here pertains to data privacy. No matter which industry you're in or where in the world you are, chances are at least some data privacy regulations apply to your company, and you could be heavily fined (often in the millions of dollars) if you're discovered to be in violation.

In this chapter, I will summarize some of the most relevant data privacy regulations. I will cover some scary but useful data breach research. Then I will introduce the concepts of governance, risk, and compliance. I'll explain why even though compliance is a must, it doesn't ensure security. I'll also go into further detail about risk management as it applies to cybersecurity and introduce threat modeling.

Data breaches are possibly the most common and destructive type of cyber incident! Preventing them and assuring compliance are essential steps.

What Are Data Breaches, and Why Are They Bad?

A data breach occurs whenever data is exposed to entities that aren't entitled to access it. A data breach could be the result of a malicious act, or it could be an accident. Breached data could be totally accessible to the general public, or it could be sold by cybercriminals to whomever is willing to buy it. Data breaches aren't exclusive to digital data either. The data in hard-copy files can also be breached. Data is data, whether it's binary code running through your CPU or printed in the books in your local library.

Because sensitive information can be printed on paper, many offices dispose of documents by putting them through a paper shredder. Some companies, such as Shred-it, exist to protect the privacy of a company's printed data. But due to the rise of computers and the internet, most data breaches expose digital data.

Data breaches are the primary threat to the confidentiality pillar of the confidentiality, integrity, and availability (CIA) triad of cybersecurity. All cyber threats affect at least one of those components; some cyber threats even affect more than one component.

One example of a data breach comes from the new strains of ransomware that emerged in the 2020s. Ransomware is a type of malware that scrambles your digital data with encryption, using a key that only the cyber threat actor has. They present a ransom note to you, often as a text file or local web page, for example, "If you want your data back, pay us $50,000 worth of Bitcoin!"

Ransomware has existed at least since the early 2000s. I saw some of the earliest ransomware during my remote tech support days, targeting Windows users and demanding a credit card number. These sorts of attacks predated the advent of cryptocurrency; Bitcoin, the first cryptocurrency, emerged in 2009.

When WannaCry spread throughout the world in 2017, it was the worst ransomware threat to that date (in terms of the number of machines infected). WannaCry was a destructive strain of ransomware that infected Windows client and server machines worldwide. The National Health Service in the United Kingdom was one of the most publicized WannaCry victims, but the malware infected millions of computers in North America, Europe, and Asia. WannaCry made thousands of businesses and institutions unable to properly operate for a while. It was a learning experience that taught companies to do a better job of backing up their computer data. With backups, companies could restore their data instead of paying the ransom and thereby funding organized crime. Ransomware has mainly targeted enterprises since then but has not affected only Windows users. But as fewer companies were willing to pay ransoms, the cybercriminals innovated. These days, some ransomware attacks will breach sensitive data to the public if a ransom isn't paid on time.

These examples show that ransomware originally threatened integrity and availability: integrity because ransomware changes the data on an infected machine without the consent of its owner, and availability because it keeps data away from its owner. Now confidentiality is often at risk as well.

Ransomware is a relatively new means of data breaches. There are also many other ways that data is breached. Here are some examples that illustrate the most common ways.

An employee has some sensitive company data on a USB thumb drive. They're allowed to have that data because they need it for work, but the thumb drive is unencrypted. It falls out of the employee's pocket while having a business lunch at a restaurant. Someone else finds it, and the data is accidentally breached.

A software developer is programming a script that accesses some sensitive data. The program is supposed to deliver the data to an entity that's allowed to have it, but the developer accidentally codes the program to share the data to a publicly accessible internet resource. This alone may not be bad, because sometimes sensitive data is supposed to go on a publicly accessible internet resource, but it should be encrypted to make sure that only authorized entities have access to it. If the developer forgets to implement the encryption or posted it accidentally, the data is available to anyone who can access the internet resource.

A cyberattacker sends a phishing email that pretends to be from a company's IT department. It says, "Something is wrong with your work PC. I need your username and password in order to fix it." The targeted employee gives the cyberattacker their credentials, either through email or the attacker's web form. Now the attacker has access to sensitive data that only employees are allowed access to, and they could sell it in a database on a dark web market.

A cyberattacker spends a lot of time finding security vulnerabilities in a company's web application. They discover that if they input certain SQL code into its web form, they can confuse the web application and obtain access to data they're not permitted to have. The back-end databases that run web applications are usually based on some sort of SQL code, and inputting malicious SQL code into a web form in order to exploit it in some way is called a *SQL injection attack*.

The multitude of means of data breaches are limited only by your understanding of information technology and your imagination. But those are some of the most common ways that they occur.

Now that you know what data breaches are, it's important to understand why they're bad.

Knowledge is power. It is the understanding of information. And data is one of the major forms of information. Data in the wrong hands empowers the wrong parties and disempowers its victims. For centuries before the invention of electronic computers, militaries would go out of their way to communicate essential information to their troops while hiding it from their enemies. They would provide the latitude and longitude and the time for a surprise attack. Communications were delivered through a secret analog code that only their troops were supposed to know. Even ancient civilizations conducted communications this way.

Long after electronic computers were invented, old-fashioned analog encryption techniques were still used in warfare. Throughout the 20th century and even today, anyone with a shortwave radio could access what enthusiasts call *numbers stations*. These shortwave radio stations would just repeat numbers or some other sort of code, and it was gibberish to anyone not in the know. We're almost certain that numbers stations were used to communicate sensitive tactical information to spies and soldiers. The intended recipients of numbers stations messages would be equipped with a one-time pad, the decryption code in written form. Usually, it would be a sheet of paper with random numbers in groups of five or more. Historians and communications experts including Simon Mason, Lewis Bush, and Bruce Schneier have confirmed this. The only reason why the function of numbers stations isn't official knowledge is because militaries and intelligence agencies haven't admitted to it. You can learn more about numbers stations here: `www.numbers-stations.com`.

The military is one example of data protection. Certainly, drug dealers do not want law enforcement to know what they're up to and will do their best to protect their own data. But law-abiding individuals and companies have their own good reasons to protect their data from being breached. You deserve privacy in your own home. Your medical records are supposed to be kept confidential between you and your medical providers. No one should know the PIN to your bank account but you. Access to your passwords for various online accounts can result in malicious access to your social media or bank account and could ruin your life.

Companies have similar reasons for keeping their data confidential. They too have sensitive financial data and authentication credentials. Businesses in the medical and insurance industries have medical data. Technology and pharmaceutical companies have research and development information that they guard closely to maintain a competitive advantage. Companies have customers, clients, and other companies within their supply chains. They have a responsibility to guard those entities' data carefully. That data impacts their everyday business and sometimes human lives.

Data breaches are destructive to businesses of all kinds. Here are some possible implications:

If customers, clients, or other stakeholders discover their sensitive data was breached through a company, they won't want to do business with that company anymore. They'll do business elsewhere if they can. This is reputation damage that's difficult for accountants to ledger or quantify, but it can cost a company millions or even billions of dollars in lost revenue.

If sensitive data that a company is handling is breached, the company can face expensive litigation. Regardless of their guilt or innocence, they need lawyers and will have to pay expensive legal fees. Sometimes if a judge finds a company guilty of negligence, they can be fined millions of dollars. And even if the company is found innocent, the legal fees alone can be similarly expensive. These lawsuits often make the news as well, furthering the damage of a company's reputation whether or not it is deserved.

Then there's regulatory compliance and its related fines. If a data breach reveals that your company is in violation of data privacy regulations, those fines can be millions of dollars or more. Sometimes fines can even be imposed without a court hearing.

Even data breaches that only cybercriminals know about can be dangerous to a company. You don't want unauthorized entities to access your bank accounts, your research and development data, or other sensitive information because criminals can use those data breaches to steal money.

You should also be concerned about identity fraud, which occurs when criminals impersonate an individual or a business. Social Security numbers and social insurance numbers, birth certificates, driver's licenses, business operational licenses, debit cards and credit cards, and many other means of government or financial identification can be used for identity fraud. For instance, if I lose my birth certificate, the person who finds it could use it to acquire a passport and credit cards in my name. The same concept applies to companies and other types of organizations. Companies have business licenses, incorporation documents, and other similar documents that are like birth certificates for businesses.

The Scary Truth Found in Data Breach Research

Now that we know what data breaches are and why they're bad, let's examine some useful research. Understanding the frequency and direct impact of data breaches is crucial to taking this immense cyber threat seriously. Because if data breaches were rare, why bother with the effort to prevent them? But data breaches are alarmingly common and tremendously destructive. Here's some proof.

Of all the data breach research that's accessible to the public, some of the data that is most useful to businesses is Verizon's Data Breach Investigations Report (DBIR).

In the 2020 Verizon DBIR, it examined 157,525 cyber incidents in 2019, of which 32,002 were possible data breaches and 3,950 were confirmed. These incidents were from 81 different countries worldwide, from businesses in a wide variety of industries and of different sizes.

Here are the statistics Verizon acquired from this data:

- 45 percent of breaches were caused by malicious actions, what it calls *hacking*.
- 22 percent of breaches were due to accidents caused by human or computer error.
- 17 percent of breaches involved malware.
- 8 percent of breaches were caused by misuse by authorized users, whether accidental or deliberate.
- 70 percent of breaches were perpetrated by external actors: anyone who doesn't work for a company.

- 55 percent of breaches involved organized criminal groups.
- 30 percent of breaches involved internal actors: employees, contractors, and even executives.
- Only 4 percent of breaches had four or more attacker actions. That means cyberattacks didn't usually require a lot of effort.
- 86 percent of malicious breaches were financially motivated.
- 43 percent of breaches involved web applications. This shows how important it is to keep web applications cyber secure.
- 27 percent of the malware used in data breaches was ransomware, an alarming new trend.
- 37 percent of breaches exploited credentials, such as usernames and passwords.
- 22 percent of breaches involved phishing.
- 72 percent of breaches involved large business victims, which the report defines as organizations with 1,000 or more employees.
- 28 percent of breaches involved small business victims, which the report defines as organizations with fewer than 1,000 employees.
- 58 percent of victims had personal data compromised.

Where do data breaches come from?

- Roughly 55 percent were caused by organized crime.
- Almost 10 percent were caused by nation-state or state-affiliated attacks. This is the definition of military cyberwarfare.
- About 10 percent were caused by systems administrators. These are people who work in the IT department.
- And about 10 percent were caused by end users. End users are anyone who is supposed to use an application or computer system, as opposed to someone who creates, develops, or administrates it. End users are often customers, but they're also sometimes employees who don't work in the IT department.

The Verizon DBIR goes into detail about the nature of data breaches, but what about the financial cost? That's important to know because it's often difficult for cybersecurity professionals to convince the executives who control a company's finances to spend money and time on preventing data breaches without showing them how much data breaches cost. For that information, it's best to look at IBM's Cost of a Data Breach Study.

Based on IBM's 2020 report, the average total cost of a single data breach incident is a whopping $3.86 million. Data breaches are most expensive in the healthcare industry, at an average of $7.13 million per incident. And the United States is the country with the most expensive data breaches, at an average of $8.64 million per incident. These costs occur through litigation, regulatory fines, lost revenue from reputation damage, and other ways as well. Show those numbers to your chief financial officer, and maybe they'll be more inclined to give your company a generous cybersecurity budget. Another disturbing revelation from IBM's report is that it takes companies an average of 280 days to identify and contain a breach. That's nearly 10 months, more than enough time for breached data to do tremendous harm to a company. Data breaches would be a lot less harmful if companies could contain them within hours.

Now it's time for my anecdote. It's difficult to determine how common data breaches are, because it seems that only a minority of data breaches become public knowledge. When you see a major data breach reported in the news, think of how many similar breaches we never find out about.

My thoughts on this are based on what I learned when I used to write about cyberattacks for online news sources. I regret that I never got to break a story—I'd only ever report stories that other people were also reporting. It's much safer legally because if you're accused of defamation, you can pass on the responsibility to the person who broke the news. Breaking a story would've done wonders for my career, and it almost happened. I could have broken the news of a massive consumer data breach.

Due to the possible legal and ethical implications, I can reveal only limited information about the breach, so here is what I can share. One day in 2018, a college student emailed me about a data breach they discovered that affected a company well known by Americans and Canadians that offers consumer products and services, but not in the tech industry. Nearly 100 million customer records were breached over a period of multiple years, without the company's knowledge. The student gave me extensive digital evidence that proved everything they told me. This evidence could be used to show that the story was worth reporting and may have been able to protect me from being sued for defamation if I reported the story. My source did the responsible thing. They showed the data to the company first, but they received no response after a month. That's when the source contacted me and shared their data. Normally I would research and write a cyberattack story in less than a day, but because of the legal and pragmatic implications of breaking a news story that could damage a company's reputation, I spent well over a week verifying data and considering the details carefully, all while working on an article draft. I had also promised my source that I wouldn't publish the story until I got the go-ahead from them.

The company contacted my source while I was working on the story, presumably because telling the company the story was ready to be reported in the media was the push it needed to take action. The company offered my source about $20,000 to keep quiet and let them handle the problem internally. It could have offered my source a lot more money than that, but the college student was broke and desperately needed the money. Plus, the company could have sued my source, costing them a lot of money even though they likely wouldn't have won in court due to how solid the evidence was.

I cooperated with my source and decided to not report the story, partly because I didn't want to interfere with my source getting the much-needed money and partly because I wanted to maintain a reputation of being a cybersecurity journalist sources can trust. To this day, I won't share any details that could be used to identify my source or the company involved. In my cybersecurity journalism days, I certainly wasn't one of the most famous people in my field, so imagine how many times sources have shared data breach discoveries with more well-known tech journalists, only for the story to be dropped for similar reasons. And think of how many data breaches only cybercriminals know about. It's terrifying to think about.

An Introduction to Common Data Privacy Regulations

There are a lot of different data privacy regulations all over the world. Some pertain to all companies in a country (or group of countries) that handle data, and others apply to specific industries, such as healthcare or financial services. Most likely, at least one set of data privacy regulations applies to your business, and the fines your organization can incur if you're found to mishandle sensitive data could be in the millions of dollars or more.

It is important that you know what these regulations are so you can start working on compliance. If you don't know which regulations apply to your company, I highly recommend consulting a legal or cybersecurity firm that deals with governance, risk management, and compliance. Paying for that consultation is money well spent that will help save your company much more money in the future.

There are many more regulations than I can address in this book, so I will introduce you to some of the most common data privacy regulations—the ones that apply to the most worldwide organizations. Some of these regulations consist of hundreds or thousands of pages of documentation, so I will cover some of the most important points as they pertain to companies and data breaches. As you engage in step 3, you should work with people who specialize in data privacy regulation compliance so you can make sure you're doing things right.

The General Data Protection Regulation

The General Data Protection Regulation (GDPR) may be the most well-known data privacy regulation in the world. It applies to organizations in all industries that handle or store data physically within the European Union (EU) and that handle or store the data of EU citizens, residents, and organizations outside of the European Union.

The GDPR was first proposed and passed in 2012. Largely due to its expensive fines, companies worldwide spent a lot of time and money in preparation for it. By May 2018, the 2012 law took effect.

To comply with the GDPR, companies are not permitted to acquire data from individuals or organizations without informed consent, and their consent can be withdrawn at any time. One of the effects of the GDPR's informed consent requirement can be seen in the increased frequency with which websites have asked for consent to use web cookies since 2018. The website could be based outside of Europe, but if there's any chance some European Union residents could be visiting the website, a smart company makes sure that they have their tracks covered.

Another requirement of the GDPR is that when an organization discovers that they've had a data breach, they have only 72 hours to report the breach to customers, even if those 72 hours include weekends or holidays. The company I nearly wrote about that was hit by the data breach would've been in deep trouble if they had European data and were caught.

The GDPR also allows for users to request a copy of the data an organization has about them. The organization must share the data with the user and must also be able to explain how it's using that data. Additionally, when the original purpose of a customer's data has been realized, they have the right to make the organization completely erase or delete that data. This is also known as the right to be forgotten.

If your organization is caught in violation of the GDPR, the fines can be severe. There are two tiers of fines, both of which are in the millions of Euros per violation. The first tier is for minor violations. The fine is €10 million, or 2 percent of the firm's worldwide annual revenue from the preceding financial year, whichever amount is higher. The second tier is for more severe violations. The fine is up to €20 million, or 4 percent of the firm's worldwide annual revenue from the preceding financial year, whichever amount is higher.

For more information about the GDPR, I recommend that you visit `https://gdpr.eu/`.

The California Consumer Privacy Act

The GDPR pertains to EU entities, and the European Union consists of 26 member states. American data privacy regulations are much more localized. Most American data privacy regulations only apply to one state or US territory. California's regulations are among the strictest, and they were largely inspired by the GDPR. The California Consumer Privacy Act (CCPA) was signed into law in June 2018. Here's some of what you should know about it.

The CCPA applies to data pertaining to California residents, with exemptions for personal health information and financial information, as those are usually covered by the California Financial Information Privacy Act or by one or more federal laws, the Health Insurance Portability and Accountability Act (HIPAA) and the Gramm-Leach-Bliley Act. Also, CCPA only applies to businesses that meet at least one of these criteria: at least $25 million in gross revenues; buys, receives, or sells the personal information of 50,000 or more consumers; or earns more than half of its annual revenue from selling consumers' personal information.

Under the CCPA, California residents have the right to know what personal data is being collected from them, to know whether their data is being disclosed to another entity, to say no to the sale of their personal data, to access their personal data, to request that an organization delete their personal data, and to not be discriminated against for exercising their rights.

If a customer's data is breached and the customer is interested in statutory damages, they must notify the business of the alleged violation. The business then has up to 30 days to remedy the violation and provide the customer with "an express written statement that the violations have been cured and that no further violations shall occur." The onus should not be on the customer to discover the violation and then make the company aware of it, but at least there's a 30-day time limit for the company to do something tangible about it.

If a business is found to be in violation of the CCPA, they can be fined up to $7,500 per intentional violation or $2,500 per unintentional violation. Those fines are minimal compared to GDPR fines, but businesses can be fined for possibly dozens of violations at a time.

For more information about the CCPA, I recommend that you visit `https://oag.ca.gov/privacy/ccpa`.

The Health Insurance Portability and Accountability Act

HIPAA is the major data privacy regulation that pertains to personal health data in all 50 US states. It was signed into law in 1996. HIPAA applies to organizations in the healthcare and insurance industries that handle the personal medical data of American residents. HIPAA is a complicated series of regulations with three major components. The Privacy Rule mandates that organizations engage in "minimum necessary data sharing." It ensures that organizations share patient data with other entities only as it's required to treat the patient or charge for medical insurance or fees. Although it may seem that news reports on a celebrity's cause of death or an American writing about their own cancer surgery on Facebook might be HIPAA violations, this is not the case. Any person can choose to share their own health information. HIPAA applies to healthcare organizations, not to individuals.

The Security Rule goes into detail about how organizations must store, share, handle, and secure patient data. Some of the cybersecurity details in HIPAA are included in the Security Rule.

The HITECH Act provides regulations for other cybersecurity requirements and expands enforcement for violations and breaches.

Especially due to how complex HIPAA is, I recommend that you visit `https://www.hhs.gov/hipaa/index.html` for more information.

The Gramm-Leach-Bliley Act

The Gramm-Leach-Bliley Act became law in 1999, and it applies to banks and other financial services organizations in all 50 US states. There are two parts of the Gramm-Leach-Bliley Act that are the most relevant to financial data privacy.

The Financial Privacy Rule requires financial institutions to provide each consumer with a privacy notice at the time the consumer relationship is established and annually thereafter. The notice must include which information is being collected, how the information is being used, how it may be shared, and how it's being protected. The consumer also has the right to opt out of allowing their information to be shared with unaffiliated parties through the Fair Credit Reporting Act. The Safeguards Rule requires financial institutions to develop a written plan to secure financial information.

Noncompliance with the Gramm-Leach-Bliley Act can result in imprisonment of up to five years and fines of up to $100,000 per violation.

There is a lot of information on the Gramm-Leach-Bliley Act, and you should visit `https://www.ftc.gov/tips-advice/business-center/privacy-and-security/gramm-leach-bliley-act` to learn more.

Payment Card Industry Data Security Standard

Payment Card Industry Data Security Standard (PCI DSS) pertains to the security of debit cards and credit cards. It's not a governmental regulation; rather, it's enforced by the Payment Card Industry Security Standards Council, a collective of many financial service providers including Visa, MasterCard, and American Express. If you operate a retail or food service business, either in old-fashioned brick-and-mortar shops or online, chances are the PCI DSS applies to your organization. The PCI DSS is an international standard.

Governance, Risk Management, and Compliance

Governance, risk management, and compliance (GRC) is a major component of business cybersecurity. GRC is a way to measure the effect and implementation of regulations, policies (including a company's own policies), and foreseeable issues when it comes to managing data.

Governance is how an organization's executives manage and direct large enterprises with hierarchies and policies. It relates to the ways a large company governs itself, ensures that policies are enforced, and ensures that they have the information necessary to make decisions and enact company strategies.

Risk management ensures that companies have a way to determine risks that impact their organization's data and other assets. Everything related to security and finances has some degree of risk. Organizations need to decide how much risk they're ready to tolerate relative to the related rewards. This is sometimes a matter of cost-benefit analysis.

Compliance is all about making sure your organization complies with regulations, such as the data privacy regulations discussed previously, other government regulations and related laws, the rules of their markets, and the rules of any applicable industry organizations in the private sector as well.

I strongly recommend that your company consult with people who specialize in GRC. If your company is large enough, you should probably employ GRC specialists as well.

More About Risk Management

The first step to effective risk management is the acceptance that everything your company does is associated with some risk, both inside and outside of cybersecurity. This includes old-fashioned financial risks as well.

As far as cybersecurity is concerned, cyber incidents will happen. Are you ready to handle them? As your company determines its risk tolerance for various factors and actions, the balance between usability and security is important to consider.

Here's an example. Online accounts can be more secure if users must provide multiple factors of authentication. The first factor can be a username with a long, complex password. Second-factor authentication often involves a temporary verification code sent to a user's phone or email that the user then needs in order to log on. Fingerprint and iris scan biometrics can be a third layer of security. A user may cooperate with three factors of authentication to log into their accounts every so often, but they likely won't continue to cooperate if they have to jump through all three hoops more than once per day. They may choose weak passwords like "12345" or "password." They may find ways to evade the other two factors or decide to use the system much less frequently than necessary, directly impacting a company's bottom line. In Silicon Valley speak, that's too much friction. A situation like this is a good example showing how a company needs to balance security with usability in their risk management process.

When risks can cost a company money, that's where cost-benefit analysis comes in. What are the costs of an action and its associated benefits? If an expense or financial risk is insufficiently beneficial, then it's not worth taking. But I'm the cybersecurity nerd, and you're the businessperson, so ideally this is one of your areas of expertise.

Threat Modeling

You probably engage in a form of threat modeling in your everyday life, even if you aren't aware of it. Threat modeling is all about anticipating risk and danger and acting in a way to mitigate it. At home, I've decided to leave a burning candle unattended for only half an hour or so; otherwise, the threat of fire is too much for me. If I'm baking something in my oven, I'll check it at least every 15 minutes or so. If there's a fire in my apartment building, I know I cannot escape through the elevator or my very high balcony. I know where each of the concrete stairwells are, and I will evacuate through the nearest stairwell that isn't obstructed by smoke or fire.

I've never driven a car, but I'm often a pedestrian. Will I jaywalk across the street? If it's Yonge Street, one of Toronto's busiest, I won't, but if it's a quaint little residential street with maybe one car per minute, I likely will.

Similar thinking applies to cybersecurity threat modeling. You must understand the possible threats that pertain to your organization and decide what you need to do about them.

Threat modeling includes prioritizing and triaging threats. Security testing, as I describe in the next chapter, will help your organization determine what your cyber threats are. That's one of the ways you can acquire information that you can use to engage in threat modeling. Once you have identified your threats, you can rank them according to how much harm they can cause your organization's data and financial assets. Your company has finite capacity to manage threats. Greater threats are the most important to address or mitigate. Then you can work on the less significant threats.

Cyber threats result in cyber incidents. In future chapters, we will address security frameworks and how to use them to develop incident response policies. We will also discuss how threats pertain to your organization's data assets and how you can manage them.

Threat modeling is possible without specific methodologies. But companies often decide that implementing a specific methodology is best suited for their needs. Carnegie Mellon University has an excellent guide to threat modeling methodologies you can find here: `https://insights.sei.cmu.edu/sei_blog/2018/12/threat-modeling-12-available-methods.html`.

The topics I've discussed in this step are ultimately facets of defensive security, everything an organization must do to defend against cyber threats. Regulatory compliance is the key component, even though it doesn't guarantee security. GRC and threat modeling are ways to apply a defensive security approach to your business.

First, you should understand which regulations apply to your business and then work on compliance. From there, you should go one step further and make sure your organization is doing everything it can to defend its data and computer networks. A proper defensive security approach goes beyond compliance and works on mitigating as many cyber threats as possible.

Chapter 4
Step 4: Frequent Security Testing

The key to properly securing your network and your organization's data is to find security vulnerabilities and remedy them. This isn't something you should just do once. Security testing and subsequent security hardening must be done on a regular basis. Not only is the cyber threat landscape constantly evolving, but your data, your network, and your computing devices are also constantly evolving. Each little bit of change can introduce a new vulnerability. You must be proactive, constant, and vigilant when it comes to the cybersecurity of your business and its precious data assets.

The problem is that a lot of companies find security testing overwhelming. This applies to businesses of all sizes and in all industries. They often don't know where to start. Sometimes IT specialists also struggle to convince *the suits* in their companies to spend money on security testing. This is what I hear from the cybersecurity testing professionals I speak with every day.

I'm here to help. In this chapter, I'll explain what security testing is, what the different types of security testing are, and what kind of security testing your company needs and why, and I'll offer tips for starting a proper security testing program in your organization.

What Is Security Testing?

Security testing involves all the different ways your organization can discover security vulnerabilities in your network. Vulnerabilities are exploited by cybercriminals, and sometimes vulnerabilities can also threaten your data accidentally, such as if an employee leaves a USB drive in a public washroom and causes a data breach.

As your organization changes policies, installs new applications, patches software, adds new devices, hires new people, and so on, new vulnerabilities can be introduced to your network. So, security testing needs to be frequent so vulnerabilities can be patched, mitigated, or otherwise remedied before they cause a security problem. Cyberattacks often cost businesses millions of dollars per incident, so a little bit of time and effort invested in regular security testing can go a long way when it comes to looking after your bottom line.

Your company's size, industry, and security maturity level will affect which kinds of security testing are appropriate for your organization. Security maturity is a measure of how advanced your organization's cybersecurity team and programs are. It takes years to build security maturity. I will explain the concept further later in this chapter. Also, a lot of security testing terminology is misused in marketing. For example, types of security testing that aren't penetration testing are often erroneously referred to as penetration testing by salespeople. We'll explore the different types of security testing here, in plain English.

Security Testing Types

If you don't have a cybersecurity background, you'll probably be surprised by how many types of cybersecurity testing there are. Your company should probably conduct multiple kinds of security tests, but not all kinds of security tests are useful for all organizations.

Security Audits

Security audits test your organization's security configuration according to a specific standard. Most of the time, a security audit is conducted based on a particular security regulation, which I described in Chapter 3. For instance, an American company in the healthcare industry may perform a security audit based on the HIPAA regulations that pertain to medical data. Some countries and industries have mandatory regulations like HIPAA, but anything that can be considered a specific security standard can be used in a security audit. For example, the Open Web Application Security Project (OWASP) is a nonprofit organization that maintains web application security standards. These are good guidelines for web application security, but they're optional. No government regulatory fines will be owed if your organization doesn't comply with them, but OWASP standards can be used in a security audit of a web application.

Security audits can impact organizations of all sizes and security maturity levels. Your security auditing will be based on which security regulations and optional standards pertain to your organization, which depend on your country and industry and which sorts of applications and features you have. I will explain security maturity later in this chapter.

Vulnerability Assessments Versus Penetration Testing

A vulnerability assessment is a way to find as many vulnerabilities in your organization as you can, in a generalized way. An effective vulnerability assessment will conclude with a report on which vulnerabilities are the most urgent to address and how to remedy them. These are frequently confused with a network vulnerability scan. But a network vulnerability scan is when an application like Metasploit Framework or Nessus is executed in a network to look for specific vulnerabilities that have been configured, whereas vulnerability assessment is a much broader category.

A vulnerability assessment may look at physical security, such as whether the doors to your datacenter are locked. If a new bug has been discovered in an operating system your organization uses, a vulnerability assessment may look at your organization's computers and see if the bug exists in how the operating system is installed and configured on them.

Although vulnerability assessments can be conducted based on physical security, your computing devices, your software, your network configurations, and your employees, there's one big difference between a vulnerability assessment and a penetration test. A vulnerability assessment tries to find as many vulnerabilities as possible without a particular goal in mind, whereas a penetration test involves behaving like a cyberattacker and performing specific simulated cyberattacks.

Frequently vulnerability assessments are erroneously marketed as penetration tests because security testing clients are more likely to be familiar with the latter term, and perhaps a penetration test sounds more serious or *sexier*. But neither type of security test is better than the other; the different types of tests are simply more appropriate in different situations.

Here's a useful way to visualize the difference between security audits, vulnerability assessments, and penetration tests. A security audit is a checklist of traits your network should have in order to comply with or conform to a security standard. Think of it as a person holding a clipboard with a long list, making check marks next to positive findings, and writing an "x" next to each negative finding. A vulnerability assessment is like an Easter egg hunt, where people try to find as many security vulnerability Easter eggs as they can in a particular environment. A penetration test involves pretending to be a cyberattacker and seeing if they can penetrate your network to find data they're not entitled to access.

If your organization has a low- to medium-level security maturity rating, you should choose to conduct vulnerability assessments rather than penetration tests. An organization without a high level of security maturity will find lots of vulnerabilities in a vulnerability assessment, whereas a more security mature network will find fewer vulnerabilities. Instead, a more security mature organization will want to focus on whether a cyberattacker will be successful if they try to do certain things, so they should perform penetration testing. Penetration tests are often called *pentests* for short. And the people who perform pentests are usually called *pentesters* or *ethical hackers*.

Red Team Testing

In the same way that people often confuse vulnerability assessments for pentesting, they often also confuse pentesters and red teamers. A red team is a dedicated offensive security group within your organization. Offensive security involves the simulated cyberattacks that pentesters and red teamers do. Only larger companies have the resources to support a red team. But if your organization is large enough for a red team, then you'll also need to have a blue team. The blue team is a group of defensive security professionals who learn about vulnerabilities from the red team and use that information to make their network more secure.

Penetration testing can be conducted by an external third-party firm that your organization hires to simulate cyberattacks or by your red team if you have one. So, penetration testing is often red team work, but not all kinds of penetration testing are red team work. I will explain the different types of pentesting third-party entities do versus the different types of penetration testing red teams do later in this chapter.

In a nutshell, red team testing is penetration testing done by a dedicated offensive security team that's internal to your organization. Usually, only companies with more than 1,000 employees have a red team, because these are people who specialize in security testing within an organization without having unrelated information technology responsibilities such as network administration. A larger company has a greater need for specific internal cyberattack simulation campaigns and more resources to support that need.

Bug Bounty Programs

Bug bounty programs are usually offered to the general public, with some conditions. They are used to find new vulnerabilities in particular software applications and hardware devices, by the company that creates the software and hardware.

A bug bounty program is a public offering: "Hey, you, clever people out there in the public, if you can find a vulnerability in

Windows 10 that Microsoft doesn't know about, show it to Microsoft and you may get paid for your discovery!"

Indeed, Microsoft is a perfect example of a company that should have a bug bounty program. First, billions of people worldwide use its products and services. Microsoft can also afford to spend millions of dollars on bug bounty rewards every year. Finally, the company has a high security maturity level. That means that when random members of the general public give Microsoft bug reports, it has a large team of software developers and cybersecurity professionals to triage those reports, determine whether the bug bounty attempts are legitimate or useful, and act upon the information they receive to develop security patches for its software.

Katie Moussouris, a friend to many of us in the cybersecurity community, developed Microsoft's bug bounty program while she worked at the company between 2010 and 2014. She went on to become the founder and CEO of Luta Security, which helps other companies with vulnerability disclosure.

The first proper bug bounty program was launched by Netscape in 1995, to welcome the public to look for bugs in the beta version of the Netscape Navigator 2.0 web browser. Those were the days. Patching software through the internet was a new concept. And as consumer internet access was a relatively new phenomenon back then, it was the earliest time that a public bug bounty program was feasible. Before internet access was common, it was difficult to deploy a public bug bounty program because the internet facilitates reporting by the general public.

These days, bug bounty rewards vary greatly, from around $100 to $1,000 for minor vulnerabilities to more than $100,000 for really critical vulnerabilities in products from some of the world's largest and most famous tech companies. If you're curious to explore bug bounty programs further, HackerOne maintains a complete list of them at `https://hackerone.com/bug-bounty-programs`. If you look at the list, you'll notice that bug bounty programs are mainly from very large tech companies.

If you're a large tech company with millions of users, a lot of development and cybersecurity staff, and a high level of security maturity, a bug bounty program might be right for you. But if you're not, trying to start one will probably cause more problems than it will solve because you won't be able to manage it. And perhaps it won't be a good idea to encourage thousands of people to find vulnerabilities in your applications.

Whether or not your company has a bug bounty program, it shouldn't be your only kind of security testing. Sometimes bug bounty programs find very useful vulnerability information, but you can't do any sort of targeted security testing that way. You can't be sure of what you may find.

What's Security Maturity?

As I've explained the different types of security testing, I've mentioned the concept of security maturity quite often. That's because it's a major factor in determining which kinds of security testing are appropriate for your organization. So, what is security maturity anyway?

Security maturity is a measure of how robust your company is when it comes to managing and preventing cyber threats and incidents. If your business doesn't have any dedicated cybersecurity specialists and security is considered to be a necessary evil in your corporate culture, then it has a low maturity level. Companies with a high security maturity have a robust security culture (which I described in Chapter 1). Security is built into everything they do, and everyone in the organization plays a part. They have a red team, a blue team, a chief information security officer (CISO), and cybersecurity professionals in a variety of roles and specialties. And if they develop software and are considering a bug bounty program, they have a team dedicated to reviewing random bug reports and to developing security patches for your applications.

It's impossible to go from having a low level of security maturity one year to a high level of security maturity the next. Developing security maturity takes time. It takes years of hiring people, training them, and *retaining them*. It takes years of fostering a strong security culture in your organization. It takes years of building, deploying, and perfecting security policies and procedures. The tips in this book from step 1 to step 8 will help your company improve your security maturity over time. It takes patience and dedication. If you make a little bit of progress toward improving your security maturity each year, then you'll be on the right track. And you should be proud of your progress.

The Basics of Security Audits and Vulnerability Assessments

A security audit is conducted when a government or industry regulator examines your company's computers and networks and goes through a checklist of traits and configurations to compare them to a specific security standard. A vulnerability assessment is a security test your company's network should perform, often to assure that you'll pass a security audit with flying colors.

A security audit is something that's done to your company, often through a government agency. You don't have control over when audits are done, but you can do the work ahead of time to make sure you'll pass one without a fine. On the other hand, *a vulnerability assessment is something your company chooses to have* to make sure your network looks secure according to a security standard-related checklist.

There are thousands of different sets of security standards that your computer network could possibly be assessed with, but data security regulations such as the ones I've outlined in Chapter 3 are the ones that are most commonly used for security audits.

Basically, if you perform a vulnerability assessment on your network based on the expectations of a regulation such as the General Data Protection Regulation (GDPR) from the European Union government, or the Health Insurance Portability and Accountability Act (HIPAA) from the United States government, you're assuring that your organization won't be subject to costly regulatory fines at some point in the near future. GDPR violations can cost tens of millions of euros, and HIPAA violations can cost $100 to $50,000 per instance. If your company isn't based in Europe or an American healthcare organization, there are likely other regulations that apply to your business, and being found in violation of those regulations can be expensive as well. It's better to spend a few thousand dollars on a vulnerability assessment to make sure you're compliant than to have to pay hundreds of thousands of dollars to the government in the event of a data breach or other sort of cyber incident.

Security regulations aren't a paradigm of cybersecurity hardiness. There are lots of types of vulnerabilities that regulatory compliance can miss. There are even lots of categories of vulnerabilities that are outside of the scope of a particular regulation or other sort of security standard. A data protection regulation might not cover ways to prevent malware infections, for example. But ensuring regulatory compliance can prevent fines and also have the added benefit of ensuring that you're security hardened from a series of potential vulnerabilities.

As I've mentioned, you may also want to have a vulnerability assessment done based on a security standard that isn't a government regulation, such as OWASP's web application security checklists. Your organization won't be fined for violating an optional security standard, but complying with an optional standard can protect your organization from the other expenses associated with cybersecurity incidents, such as lost productivity and reputation damage.

I highly recommend having a third party conduct a vulnerability assessment to review your network and advise you on which security standards are useful or applicable to your company's network. Then you can order assessments that are appropriate for your particular business. It's much cheaper to hire out your own vulnerability assessments to ensure compliance than to face expensive fines if the government decides to audit your business. Every time a major change is made to your network, such as changing your operating system or integrating a new cloud provider, you should seriously consider having a vulnerability assessment conducted. Significant changes to your network can introduce many new security vulnerabilities, no matter what you do. It's also prudent to conduct an assessment once every year or two. I combine those two recommendations into my golden rule: conduct a vulnerability assessment whenever a major change is made to your network or once every 19 months or so, whichever is more frequent.

Log Early, Log Often

The most important thing your company can do to facilitate a vulnerability assessment and to make sure you can pass an audit is to create and retain as many logs as possible. Network security appliances such as firewalls and routers can all be logged. Each computer on your network regardless of its purpose or operating system can be logged. If you have data storage or printer devices on your network, they can be logged. Many of your applications within the operating systems of your computers can be logged. You should assign every employee who works with your computers and network a unique user account. With that, everything your employees do in your computer network can be logged. Whether your employees are at the company workplace or working from home, they can be logged. And if your organization uses a cloud network from a provider such as AWS or Microsoft Azure, your use of those platforms can also be thoroughly logged. All of your computer activity, wherever in the world it occurs, can be logged as long as it's communicating with your network in some way.

If your network isn't set up to create logs for as much activity as possible, you should establish thorough logging *as soon as possible*. Don't hesitate. Nothing should happen in your network without there being a record somewhere that can be referenced in an audit. Your network security professionals can help you with this endeavor.

It's best to retain those logs for at least a couple of years. Store them on both your local network and your cloud service if at all possible.

Once you've established thorough and automatic logging, you'll want to cut through the tedium of it all. A human being would be overwhelmed and likely bored to read thousands of pages of "user logged on, user executed these applications, user logged off." That's where log analysis software comes in. A network security professional can help you find the log analysis software that's best for your organization. This software allows your security specialists to make sense of the logs. Furthermore, logging doesn't only assist with passing security audits. Logging will also help your defensive security specialists prevent cybersecurity incidents and respond to cybersecurity incidents when they occur.

If you have a large company and thousands of computers, then you should really consider acquiring a security information and event management system (SIEM). Your defensive security specialists can route all of your network logs through your SIEM, which can be configured with correlation rules that will alert your defensive security specialists when possible cyber incidents are happening, according to certain patterns in your logs.

Prepare for Vulnerability Assessments and Security Audits

Creating and keeping lots and lots and lots of logs will help your organization with both vulnerability assessments and security auditing. The latter can often be an unpleasant surprise.

Here are my other tips for preparing for vulnerability assessments and security audits:

- Review your information security and data security policies. These policies establish your company's rules for how data should be managed. Sometimes this data is very sensitive, such as financial credentials. Other times, data that's delivered through a network may seem unimportant or innocuous, such as an employee's recreational web surfing, but those network packets often contain authentication data that a cyberattacker could use to maliciously penetrate your company's network. All computer data should be relevant to your policies. Also, sometimes noncomputer data can put your network at risk. Your employee could tell someone who says they're your company's tech support (but is actually a cybercriminal) their username and password over the phone, a typical phone phishing exploit. Or sensitive company data could be printed on paper and fall into the wrong hands. So, your data security policies should be comprehensive. I'll explain how to protect the security of all kinds of data in step 6.

- Centralize your security policies. You should keep all of your policies in one place so if a security tester or auditor asks for the record of a particular policy, you can find them all easily. You may have policies for which types of employees should have access to which data assets. You may have disaster recovery and business continuity plans in case of a natural disaster. You may have bring-your-own-device policies that determine how employees may use their own phones or laptops with your company network. You may have cyber incident response plans. The list goes on. Write everything down in useful documentation, and keep it all handy as needed.
- Review all of the security regulations that apply to your business. These are the regulatory compliance standards I outlined in Chapter 3. These are the standards by which your organization may be audited. You need to know the details of these regulations to help ensure compliance.
- Record information about how your computer networks are structured. This applies whether your network is entirely on your premises, through a cloud provider, or a hybrid of the two. Have your IT networking professionals create and update network diagrams accordingly, lay out your network assets, and describe how they work together. You will need to have this information readily available for review so that whoever is vulnerability assessing your network doesn't have to waste time figuring out the structure of your networks themselves. Having these diagrams also ensures that you have full visibility into your network so none of your precious data assets are missed.
- Outline your cybersecurity team. Every single person in your organization who has any cybersecurity-related responsibilities whatsoever, from network administrators to your CISO, should be described in a document. It should include all roles and

responsibilities for each of them. If a vulnerability assessor or security auditor has to trace a *buck*, it must *stop* somewhere, as in "the buck stops here."

A Concise Guide to Penetration Testing

As I have mentioned, if your organization has at least a medium level of security maturity, penetration testing can be a great way to improve your cybersecurity. Whereas a vulnerability assessment is conducted by going through a checklist, a penetration test is conducted by simulating cyberattacks. Your penetration testers get to pretend to be the bad guys.

Essentially, there is one major difference between a malicious cyberattack and a pentest. That difference is consent. A cyberattacker will try to penetrate your network without your consent. A pentester will try to penetrate your network according to what you permit them to do. There must be a legal document and work order between your organization and your pentester. That document will describe in detail what your pentesters are allowed to do and what they're not allowed to do. Your pentesters might only be permitted to pentest a particular network segment. There might be types of exploits they're allowed to simulate and types of exploits they're forbidden from simulating. This is important to have in signed legal documentation because pentests can interrupt the functioning of your computer network. For example, your employees might be unable to access a server that a pentester is trying to break into. You might want your employees to stop using particular network resources while they're being pentested. And there might be types of pentesting you want to avoid altogether because they'd be too harmful to do. Also, a particular scope should be defined for a pentest that identifies which computers will be tested, how they should be tested, and so on. Your security specialists will want to test certain kinds of cyberattacks if they're looking for certain kinds of vulnerability information. Will your web application pass a scan with OWASP ZAP (a web application vulnerability scanner)? Can your employees be fooled by social engineering tests that involve ways a cyberattacker could deceive them in order to acquire information they're not entitled to? Can your datacenter be physically broken into? These are all kinds of vulnerabilities a pentester may look for when they simulate a cyberattack, and you need to decide what you'll permit them to do. If they pentest outside of the scope of your agreement, then they are actually cyberattacking, regardless of their good intentions.

As I've mentioned, it's important to make sure you have at least a medium level of security maturity for a pentest to be a good idea in the first place. If your company is only a couple of years into the process of building cybersecurity resilience, then it's too soon for a pentest. At that point, you should only conduct vulnerability assessments. If you try to pentest in a low security maturity environment, your network will have way too many holes for simulating cyberattacks, and it's possible that every penetration attempt will be successful. Your network and your employees then won't be able to manage the effects. First, you need to ensure that most of the common sorts of vulnerabilities have already been prevented or mitigated. A pentest is effective only when you're ready to look for vulnerabilities that a thorough vulnerability assessment may miss. A pentest could knock some of your servers offline unexpectedly. Could your network and organization deal with that? Once you've assured that you have a robust security team and vulnerability assessments find very few problems, that's an indication that your network may be ready for penetration testing.

Penetration Testing Based on Network Knowledge

One way to classify pentests is according to how much knowledge a pentester has of your network. These methods include black-box, white-box, and gray-box testing.

Black-box testing is done when your pentesters have little to no knowledge of what your network is like. They won't know which operating systems and applications you use. They won't know how many computers and networking devices you have. They won't know the details of how your computers are used. They won't know anything about your network design. They might even be ignorant of which departments and roles your company has.

Black-box testing is done from the perspective of an external cyberattacker. Therefore, black-box testing can be done only when your company hires an external security testing firm in order to do it. Anyone who has ever worked in your company will have a little bit of knowledge of your network, even if not part of your IT department. Black-box testing is conducted to test your cyber resilience in the wake of a bad guy who knows little about your company but wants to do bad things. These types of cyberattack attempts will probably happen to your company, so you need to see if you're prepared for them. External cyberattacks are usually the first kind of cyberattack a layperson thinks about, such as some nasty ransomware going around the internet or a cybercrime group that tries to steal financial data from the point-of-sale devices of well-known retailers. Sometimes, external cyberattackers target your company specifically. Other times, malicious external attacks are promiscuous, such as when a cyberattacker wants to distribute malware through the internet and make it infect as many computers as it can.

Because the penetration tester has limited network knowledge, black-box pentests are the quickest to run. The duration of the pentest largely depends on their ability to find and exploit vulnerabilities in your network's outward-facing services. But if the pentesters can't breach the perimeter of your network, internal service vulnerabilities may remain undiscovered and unpatched.

White-box testing is done with significant prior knowledge of your network. White-box pentesters will know or have access to information about all of your operating systems and applications, all of your computers and devices, how your network is designed and configured, and so on. The challenge with white-box testing is to analyze the massive amount of data available to identify potential points of weakness, so it's the most time-consuming type of penetration testing.

White-box pentesters simulate cyberattacks from the perspective of someone who's inside of your organization's IT department. There are two major reasons why white-box pentesting is useful. Internal cyberattacks are a real threat to organizations of all kinds. They're typically done by disgruntled employees and contractors who may want revenge if they feel the company has mistreated them. A white-box pentest will see if your network could succumb to such an internal cyberattack. The other reason why white-box testing is useful is because it is more effective at finding internal service vulnerabilities. The testers are already inside of your network perimeter, so they don't have to spend hours or days trying to breach it.

There are two major ways to approach a white-box pentest. You could hire an external entity to perform it, as you would with a black-box test, but then you would have to give them all of the information your network administrators may have about your network. The other approach is to have a red team in your organization perform white-box pentests internally. If your company is large enough, you can hire offensive security professionals whose sole responsibility is to conduct internal white-box pentesting campaigns. If there's a hot new cyber threat going around, like 2017's WannaCry ransomware, your red team could try to simulate that particular cyberattack within your network. When your offensive security specialists become aware of any significant new cyber threat, they can design pentesting campaigns accordingly.

Then there's gray-box testing. *Gray-box testing* is the middle ground between white-box testing and black-box testing. White-box testing is done with lots of knowledge, and black-box testing is done with pretty much zero knowledge. Gray-box testing is done with a little bit of knowledge. As a white-box tester has the perspective of someone in your IT department, and a black-box tester has the perspective of a completely external cyberattacker, a gray-box tester has the perspective of an employee who doesn't work in your IT department, such as a receptionist or a data entry clerk.

As I mentioned, black-box tests are relatively quick, and white-box tests are relatively lengthy in duration. When you don't have enough time for a white-box test but you want your testers to be more likely to find internal service vulnerabilities, a gray-box test could be a useful compromise between the two extremes. Your gray-box testers will be given the network privileges equivalent to an employee who doesn't work in your IT department. If your organization has just recently hired a red team or this is your first penetration test, a gray-box test could be the best kind of pentest to start with.

Penetration Testing Based on Network Aspects

The other way to classify pentests is according to which aspects of your network are being tested.

Some offensive security professionals specialize in *application pentesting*. A lot of people who start their careers by participating in bug bounty programs go on to specialize as application pentesters. These professionals understand computer programming languages and application development with considerable expertise. Application pentesters will pretend to be a cyberattacker by trying to break a web application or privilege and escalate through your server software to acquire access only an administrator should have, such as rewriting, deleting, or reconfiguring data. Application pentesting is an entire penetration testing specialty. Any sort of pentesting designed to break into software applications of any kind falls into this category.

Physical pentesting simulates cyberattacks based on your organization's physical security. Cyberattackers don't just try to hack software and hardware directly. Sometimes they need to acquire physical access to your computing devices. A physical pentester may try to break locks, remove doors, climb through your ventilation system, or tailgate an employee to access an area of your building that's restricted. Physical security is a frequently overlooked aspect of cybersecurity. It would be prudent for your organization to do everything possible to secure your buildings to make sure a cyberattacker can't physically touch your computers. Some types of cyber exploits can't be done through the internet; they can be done only if an attacker has direct physical access. When your organization has some security maturity, you should look for pentesting specialists who know how to break into rooms and datacenters.

Social engineering pentesting is all about the art of human deception. Remember the story of Kevin Mitnick from Chapter 1? He was able to cyberattack his victims by fooling company employees. Real cyberattackers frequently fool human beings in their exploits. Your employees have privileged access to your computer systems, and human beings are imperfect, even the smartest of us out there. A social engineering pentester may try to call your employees to trick them in to giving them information they're not entitled to have. Or they may try to phish your employees by creating emails, websites, or social media messages that imitate trusted entities such as banks or other companies in your organization's industrial supply chain.

What is phishing? Phishing is when a cyberattacker pretends to be a trusted entity in order to acquire information they're not allowed to have. Here are some classic examples of phishing. A cyberattacker could create a website that's a near perfect replica of a real bank's online banking website. A victim thinks they're logging into their bank's website to conduct financial services, but they're actually giving a cyberattacker their online banking username and password, which the attacker can use to steal money from their victim. Sometimes when cyberattackers phish, they impersonate government agencies, law enforcement, consumer service companies, or companies your organization works with.

Deceptive emails, websites, text messages, or social media messages are one of the most common ways that cyberattackers acquire access to their targets through phishing. When phishing is done through a phone call, it's called *vishing*. It's often much easier to trick a human being who already has privileged access than try to find an obscure software vulnerability to remotely exploit, so social engineering vulnerabilities should always be considered when you security harden your network. I will go into detail about how to security harden your organization from social engineering attacks in Chapter 7.

While your company engages in social engineering pentests, there's one important trend you must be mindful of. When pentesters conduct simulated phishing campaigns with emails or text messages, sometimes they have engaged in unethical behavior in their simulated cyberattacks. Here are two particular examples of unethical social engineering penetration tests.

In the wake of the coronavirus pandemic, people are understandably anxious and eager to be vaccinated. Some pentesters have pretended to be government agencies or medical clinics that are conducting vaccination. ("Give me your health insurance information so we can vaccinate you as soon as possible!") This is a terrible idea for social engineering pentesting. Your employees will eventually find out that it was a trick to test their susceptibility to being scammed. What if a few months down the road, a real vaccination clinic calls them? They're going to be distrustful, and they may avoid being vaccinated. You should never do anything in a pentest that could hinder our global effort to fight a deadly pandemic. This is an example of unethical pentesting.

Here's another example of unethical social engineering pentesting I've heard about recently. Due to a global recession, there are lots of financially desperate people. Organizations have employees who are eager for social assistance money from the government so they can pay their bills and buy food. Some pentesters have pretended to be government agencies offering survival money in their phishing campaigns. Your pentesters should never be this unethical. Preying on financial desperation can result in terrible consequences.

As Rapid7 chief research officer HD Moore says:

> A lie about leaving your keys on your desk may be appropriate, but a story about a traumatic accident is likely to cause long-term mistrust when it turns out to be false. You never want to put your employees into a situation where they feel like they are in harm's way. I have heard stories of a client tackling a security tester because they followed someone through a security door.

Remember, your pentesters are just pretending to be the bad guy. They shouldn't actually become a bad guy by causing your employees grief.

Frequent security testing is absolutely crucial when it comes to keeping your company cybersecure. You won't know how to improve your security posture without it. And security testing is something your company must do frequently because your computer networks always change over time and the cyber threat landscape is always evolving.

This is a step you must not ever forget. Find your network's vulnerabilities before cyberattackers find them.

Security Leaders on Security Maturity

The concept of security maturity is an inexact science, even though there are many security maturity models. To better grasp the concept, it helps to consider the views of security professionals who have dealt with security maturity development firsthand. I asked them how an organization can build security maturity. They stressed the importance of first determining the current level of security maturity and understanding your company's risk. Once you know where you are, you determine where you want to be. Nav Bassi suggests the following:

> Pick an appropriate security framework for the organization, and then benchmark against the framework to identify the gaps. Document how the gaps contribute to organizational risk and identify the ones that are the most significant risks in terms of probability and impact. Then, develop a plan to address the gaps for these risks, making justifications for the investments based on the risks.

Most leaders suggest using a well-known risk-based framework to help you identify your risks and find your *starting point*. Then, you can build the program around that framework. Marchany then recommends tackling your risks:

> You begin by addressing your critical risk and when your security program is effective at reducing these critical risks you begin to address high risks, then medium risks, and so on. As you go down the risk levels, you continue to mature your security.

Christopher Maulding focuses on the budgetary aspect of establishing security maturity and recommends a *crawl*, *walk*, *run* methodology: "Start with user awareness training, develop it in house, then move to phishing." He suggests using an open-source tool, if necessary, as long as you put in the work to make sure it does what you want it to do.

Once a company begins to establish their security maturity, they need to understand when they have enough security maturity for pentesting. According to Mitch Parker:

> If they are capable of building defenses for common issues identified in the risk management framework and are able to demonstrate being able to detect and respond to attacks, along with holding business owners accountable for addressing them, then they are ready for pentesting.

Marchany recommends having a security program in place and then performing "a basic cybersecurity assessment or review by an independent party. An IT audit or cybersecurity firm is a great starting point."

Dean has a more simplified approach:

> The way I see it, if you have a production website on the internet, you are ready to have that asset pentested. As for IT infrastructure, is there a Windows network in place? You are ready to have that pentested.

Security Testing Is Crucial

Frequent security testing is absolutely crucial when it comes to keeping your company cybersecure. You won't know how to improve your security posture without it. And security testing is something your company must do frequently because your computer networks always change over time and the cyber threat landscape is always evolving.

This is a step you must not ever forget. Find your network's vulnerabilities before cyberattackers find them.

Chapter 5
Step 5: Security Framework Application

It's inevitable: cyber incidents will happen. In defensive security, we should do our best to security harden our computer networks and applications as well as we can. But for your business to thrive in the 21st century, you must be ready to act when a cyberattack occurs. A quick, thorough, and effective incident response will help keep your organization successful in the years and decades to come.

In Chapter 2, I discussed how you can build a good security team for companies of all sizes and in all industries. If your business has fewer than 100 people, you'll probably have just one or two people in your IT department, and they would handle all of your in-house computer operation, administration, and maintenance needs. At the other end of the spectrum are large companies with more than 10,000 people that can support a robust IT department and security operations center. How your organization prepares for and responds to incidents will depend on how many people are on your team and the size of your computer networks.

If your company has any sort of computer network, you should have a computer security incident response team (CSIRT).

Remember I mentioned in Chapter 1 how a strong security culture involves everyone in your company, not just your IT department? Your CSIRT should also have some people from outside of IT. An effective CSIRT consists of network administrators, other IT people, a legal specialist, and a PR specialist. The latter roles do not require IT credentials or experience; instead, the people in those roles can help your company manage the legal and publicity consequences of cyber incidents. Law degrees, media, and marketing experience are useful for your CSIRT, and they're often necessary.

This chapter will discuss incident response procedures, provide guidelines for delegating a CSIRT, and explain why security frameworks can be helpful.

What Is Incident Response?

A cybersecurity-minded company will first accept that cyber incidents will happen, and then they will establish a series of steps that they deploy in responding to them. This is true whether or not your organization chooses to base your incident response policies and procedures on a formal security framework. All effective incident response plans are conducted in a cycle based on the following phases.

Preparation

First, your organization *prepares* for cyber incidents. You design your incident response plan. Then you train your employees on how they should act in the event of a cyber incident. In the preparation phase, you must make sure there's funding and company approval for every part of your incident response plan. Security hardening your systems costs money, and it is essential that your company be on board with your entire incident response, from the computer technical facets to the legal and administrative facets.

Another important part of the preparation phase is ensuring that the members of your organization's CSIRT know whom to contact and how to contact them when particular cyber incidents happen. This might be different depending on the nature of the indication of compromise (a clue there may be a cyber incident, in any form it could take) and the nature of the incident itself.

Once you have an incident response plan, the next part of the preparation phase involves training. Security training is something you should conduct on a regular basis, perhaps a couple of times per year, rather than something you just do once. That's because human beings can be forgetful—it's our nature. If you've ever studied for an exam and then forgotten its curriculum years later, then you can understand why repetition and reminders are a good idea.

Incident response training is a component of your overall security training. During incident response training, your organization may choose to conduct drills of particular cyber incident scenarios. Data breaches are one of the most common and costly types of incidents, so you may base your drill on that. A data breach is when your company's sensitive and internal data gets exposed to cyber attackers or the public. This could be anything from your company email to your customer's financial records and authentication credentials. I would also recommend drilling ransomware and denial-of-service scenarios too.

Ransomware is malware that maliciously encrypts your company's data with a decryption key that only the cybercriminal has. The cybercriminal will try to extort a ransom from your company in order for you to get your files back. More and more companies are doing a better job of backing up their precious data, so they're less likely to pay the ransom. So now we're seeing some ransomware that threatens to breach your data to the public as an additional scare tactic. Having effective data backups is a good idea, but it's no longer sufficient protection from the growing ransomware threat.

Denial-of-service attacks are another common type of cyber incident. Some organizations face multiple denial-of-service attacks each week. A denial-of-service attack is when a cyberattacker overwhelms your servers with data, causing them to cease operation. Your web servers and other kinds of network servers need to stay up and running in order for your company to do business.

Denial-of-service attacks are also often a means of facilitating more destructive cyberattacks, by distracting your security devices and people. So, denial-of-service attacks are a frequent annoyance, but they're important to respond to effectively.

Identification or Analysis

After preparation, the next phase is usually described as *identification* or *analysis*, depending on the security framework you're implementing. This is what happens when a person in your organization sees an indication of compromise (IoC) for the first time. Not all IoCs are symptoms of an actual cyber incident; some may be false alarms. But they must all be investigated thoroughly so that no cyberattacks ever evade detection.

A successful cyberattack, such as one involving spyware, ransomware, or a data breach, could cost your company millions of dollars. The expense of these attacks is usually incurred through a combination of regulatory fines, litigation costs, lost productivity, network downtime, and reputation damage. The damage to your organization's reputation can result in customers and clients choosing to take their money elsewhere; this is a loss that's difficult for accountants to quantify.

Some IoCs are detected through network security appliances such as firewalls and other anomaly detection systems. Artificial intelligence technology will determine whether network or application activity is normal or malicious through algorithms and machine learning. Sometimes computers make mistakes. It's up to the human beings in your organization to look at the logs their network devices generate and make a judgment call. Sometimes corporate networks use a security information and event management system (SIEM). SIEM is technology that can be configured with correlation rules to process all of a network's logs and alert defensive security professionals when something doesn't look right. Organizations that have the resources to support a security operations center usually have a SIEM, whereas smaller companies typically don't. Humans often have to tweak and adjust firewalls, antivirus, and SIEM correlation rules so that no cyber incidents are missed, while avoiding having so many false positive alerts that they're distracted from doing useful work. Leave the configuration of network security technology to the professionals, but do understand all IoCs must be investigated.

Other ways IoCs can appear include suspicious emails, antivirus alerts, or employees encountering technical problems with their computing devices. For instance, one of your employees outside of your IT department could notice their PC is running much more slowly than usual, or a ransom note from ransomware could appear on their screen. Any way that a cyber incident can be seen is an IoC. Your CSIRT gets warnings from your IT department, but the warning could also come from someone who isn't a computer technician. Your CSIRT could learn about an IoC from your receptionist or your HR manager, for example. The first person to spot an IoC could be anyone who uses your computer systems, even one of your customers.

In the identification or analysis phase, all IoCs must be taken seriously and investigated. Think of it this way. These days, most people with breast cancer survive if the symptoms are spotted early and they get proper medical treatment as soon as possible. The earlier breast cancer is detected and treated, the greater the likelihood of survival is. But if breast cancer is spotted too late, it's often fatal. The same principle applies to cyberattacks. If a cyber incident is spotted early, it may cause your network some harm and cost your company some money. But cyber incidents that are spotted and acted upon too late can be a lot more harmful and cost a lot more money to deal with. This is why the identification/analysis phase is so crucial to your incident response.

Containment, Mitigation, or Eradication

The next phase is *containment, mitigation, or eradication*. This is when your CSIRT makes sure that a cyber incident is stopped in its tracks, doing as little damage as possible. This phase makes the timeliness of the detection phase so important.

The steps taken in this phase will differ according the nature of the cyberattack. Here's a malware example: Viruses and worms are malware that are designed to spread from device to device. If a virus or worm infects one computer in your network, it will spread to other computers in your network if it isn't stopped. Some malware could be transferring sensitive financial information to a cyberattacker's computer over the internet, whereas other malware could stop computers from operating entirely. It's bad enough if malware infects one computer, but if it infects dozens or hundreds of computers on your network, the damage will be much worse. The goal of a CSIRT in this example is to find the infected computer and remove its malware or find some other way to stop it from spreading through your network.

Malware containment is one way to resolve an identified cyberattack. If the incident doesn't involve malware or if it's a sophisticated cyberattack that involves a lot more than just malware, there could be lots of other steps that need to be taken here. The concept is the same: a cyberattack damaged your computer network, so you must stop the damage from spreading and from getting worse. For example, network administrators may decide to remove a computer from your network until its malware is removed so the malware isn't spread to other computers.

Containment is stopping the cyberattack from getting worse. Eradication is getting rid of it. For instance, your IT team may remove malware from an infected machine. Some security frameworks have these as separate phases, whereas others combine the two phases.

Recovery

The next phase is *recovery*, which involves fixing the damage that was done and restoring your computer systems to how they were before the cyberattack. If ransomware corrupted the data on your computers, recover the data from your backups. If servers went offline, repair them and bring them back online. If parts of your network had to be deliberately suspended in order to contain a cyberattack in a previous phase, this is the time to restore operation to those parts. If your software has vulnerabilities that allowed the cyber incident to happen, this is the time to install patches from your software vendor or to make and install your own patches if your company develops its own software. If a server room door was damaged because a cyberattacker physically broke into your facility, this is the time to fix or replace the door. A successful recovery will make sure your business is up and running as usual as soon as possible.

Sometimes cyber incidents become public knowledge, perhaps reported in the news. ("Company X Hit with Massive Data Breach, 100 Million Customer Records Exposed!") This is why it's often necessary to have public relations specialists in your CSIRT. They could respond or advise you on how to respond to media inquiries in order to repair the harm done to your company's reputation.

Big cyberattacks can also result in lawsuits. If customers, clients, or stakeholders in your supply chain sue your company for negligence, it can get expensive, even if a judge rules that your company did nothing wrong. Lawyers are expensive, and the cost adds up the more hours you need to hire their services. A lawsuit a litigator loses can still cost your organization thousands or millions of dollars in legal fees as a defendant.

A legal specialist on your CSIRT can sometimes help prevent your company from getting involved in a lengthy, expensive lawsuit. But if a lawsuit can't be avoided, then your CSIRT legal specialists may be able to help make the judge rule in your favor. Sometimes instead of a lawsuit, your organization may simply be hit by fines for violating data protection or related regulations. Legal assistance may be able to help your organization pay a smaller fine than you otherwise would. In any case, make sure any legal advice your company receives comes from someone with legal credentials and experience with the areas of law that impact your company.

Post-incident

The final phase is when your CSIRT learns from the incident and takes steps to reduce the likelihood of it happening again. Sometimes this phase is called *post-incident* or *lessons learned*. This phase often involves making changes to your company's security policies or procedures. You may have to instruct your employees on better security behavior. Sometimes your whole incident response plan may change. Think of it this way. Everyone makes mistakes. If you learn from your mistakes and avoid repeating them, then some good can come from the mistake. It's a way of turning lemons into lemonade. But if your organization skips this phase, then you won't be better off in the end. The post-incident phase can make your company's security posture stronger, so forgetting it is a bad idea.

When the incident is over, your CSIRT needs to return to the first phase, preparation, to make sure you're ready for future incidents and to detect and act when they happen. Effective incident response is a cycle, whether or not you follow a formal security framework.

Your Computer Security Incident Response Team

I've mentioned a bit here and there about some of the types of people who should be in your CSIRT. Let's examine CSIRTs in more detail here. As you prepare your organization for cyber incidents, delegating your CSIRT properly can make all the difference. It's like making a first-aid kit. You need to make sure your first-aid kit has all the tools and supplies you need if an injury or medical accident occurs. Your CSIRT is your human first-aid kit for cyber incidents. CSIRTs consist of different types of people with different responsibilities and different areas of expertise.

Larger companies often have a security operations center (SOC). This is a department that watches your network for IoCs, monitors the data that a SIEM produces through analyzing the logs of your network devices, and handles calls and inquiries from people in other parts of your company if they notice something suspicious on their end. If your organization is large enough to have your own SOC, then everyone who works in your SOC should be part of your CSIRT.

If your company is a small or medium-sized business, the technological line of defense in your CSIRT should be your network administrators and anyone else who handles the day-to-day operations of your network. If your business has just one or two IT people, then they're your CSIRT technicians.

Regardless of the size of your organization, whoever oversees the technical operation of your network every day is your CSIRT tech team. These are the people who spot when a cyberattacker is trying to breach your firewall, detect malware, or receive a phone call from a nontechnical employee when they say their computer isn't working properly. There must be some people with IT and computer networking expertise in your CSIRT. These are your noble geeks. Cyber incidents are an IT matter, and these people should understand technology well enough to help detect, mitigate, contain, and recover from them.

The CSIRT leader is responsible for running your CSIRT. Everyone else in your CSIRT reports to them. The leader makes the final decisions about incident response protocols, policies, and procedures. The leader assures that everyone else is doing their jobs properly. Whatever happens in your incident response, the buck stops with them.

Your chief information security officer (CISO), your chief information officer, or your chief technology officer may take the leadership role, depending on which of these executives you have and who is most senior in cybersecurity matters. If your organization is so small that you have none of those roles in your company, then the most senior IT person should take the lead.

The second in command is your CSIRT incident leader. While the leader handles the administrative stuff, the incident leader deals with the details of your incident response. They coordinate individual responses to incidents. The network administrators and other technical roles in your CSIRT report to them. If your organization has a SOC, your SOC manager would be perfect for the incident leader role. Otherwise, the role could be delegated to the person with the most computer networking experience.

Everyone else in your CSIRT who is technical will be responsible for how incidents impact the area their role pertains to, and they report to your incident leader. For example, if your company has datacenters in two different cities, the technical staff in each datacenter is responsible for responding to its incidents.

Then there are the nontechnical roles in your CSIRT. These people fall into one of two categories: public relations (PR) or legal. An effective CSIRT will have both roles filled because cyber incidents often cause reputation damage or result in fines or litigation.

If your organization has a dedicated PR person, they're the obvious choice for the incident PR role. If your organization is too small to have a dedicated PR person, you may work with a third-party PR agency to include someone who works in an external organization. That external PR person may not do work for your company every day, but they should understand what their responsibilities are if a cyber incident occurs. They should be ready for you to call or email when your incident leader is concerned about how a cyberattack may affect your company's reputation. They may need to send out press releases explaining how your company handled an incident and reassuring customers.

Large companies often have legal departments, including lawyers and paralegals who are directly employed by the organization. The head of the legal department is the clear choice to lead the CSIRT's legal response. Smaller companies may hire lawyers only as needed. If that's the case, make sure you've chosen a lawyer to call when cyber incidents lead to possible legal problems. They should understand their legal role in the CSIRT, even if they work only if you're being sued. The CSIRT incident leader is often a lawyer or CSIRT legal lead's direct contact in your organization, especially if an incident is relatively minor. But if a legal matter impacts company policies or procedures, your overall CSIRT leader may be their point of contact.

Cybersecurity Frameworks

A security framework is a set of standards for designing and implementing your cyber incident response policies. The most commonly used frameworks worldwide are the NIST Cybersecurity Framework, the ISO 27000 Cybersecurity Frameworks, the CIS Cybersecurity Framework, and the COBIT Cybersecurity Framework. Your organization may choose to implement one of those frameworks. If you're creative, you may even choose to base your incident response policies on more than one framework. Implementing security frameworks is usually optional, especially in the private sector, but it's often a good idea. Here, we'll discuss all of these most popular frameworks in a nutshell—their up sides as well as some constructive criticism that the cybersecurity community has about them.

NIST Cybersecurity Framework

The National Institute of Standards and Technology (NIST) Cybersecurity Framework is possibly the most popular security framework. The NIST is America's foremost technological standards body. They saw a need to formalize security policies for when cyber incidents impact critical infrastructure, such as power plants, hospitals, and telecommunication companies. Organizations outside of these industries also often implement the NIST Cybersecurity Framework, but it was originally invented to handle incidents to critical infrastructure—where cyber incidents could threaten human lives.

NIST made an executive order to develop a cybersecurity framework in February 2013. By February 2014, one year after the executive order, NIST Cybersecurity Framework version 1.0 was released. The framework had a significant effect on managing the cybersecurity of critical infrastructure throughout the United States, and then to other countries as well. As time went on, the framework started to become adopted by industries outside of critical infrastructure also, such as retail and public administration.

By April 2018, version 1.1 of the NIST Cybersecurity Framework was released. This new version benefited from lessons learned in implementing the first version. The most significant additions to the latest version of the framework are in the areas of authentication and identity, self-assessing cybersecurity risk, managing cybersecurity within the supply chain, and vulnerability disclosure. As of this writing, the most popular cybersecurity framework isn't even a decade old yet, but already it has had a major influence on how organizations around the world handle cyber incidents.

Here are the phases in the NIST Cybersecurity Framework, similar to the incident response cycle I described earlier.

Identify

The first phase is *Identify*. You can't protect what you can't see. So, the first function is all about identifying all of the important resources your organization must protect. Risk management starts by identifying the subjects of risk, such as servers, data, and applications. Which threats do they face, and what's a manageable level of risk for your business or institution? These subjects of risk are the assets to your organization.

The NIST Cybersecurity Framework considers your organization's assets to be both physical and in software form and recommends that you establish an asset management program for them. Asset management is one of the five main tasks of the identify function.

Sometimes organizations have hybrid networks in which an on-premises component and a cloud services component are integrated into one network. Other organizations might only have an on-premises network or one that is almost entirely in the cloud, with only client machines on the premises. Whichever form your organization's network takes, you must consider each server machine and networking appliance to be one of your assets if it's important to the functioning of your business.

Cloud providers such as AWS or Google Cloud Platform consider their responsibility to be their cloud infrastructure, leaving your organization responsible for your applications and data within their cloud infrastructure. If your organization's network is partly or completely in the cloud, you will have to consider this separation of responsibilities in the design of your asset management program.

You have operating systems and applications that are assets. You have servers, clients, data storage, and networking devices that are assets. Your organization's data is a crucial asset, too.

Your CISO and security stakeholders must take inventory of all of these assets and determine which are the most important to your organization's daily business processes. Asset management can be prioritized from there.

The next task of the identify function is to determine your organization's business environment. Your business may exist as a component in a supply chain. For example, one company produces steel. The next company buys the steel and manufactures it into automobile components. The next company buys the automobile components and uses them to manufacture cars. Then the last company buys the cars and sells them to consumers through their auto dealership. The companies within this supply chain are interdependent. A cyber incident that affects the steel producer could impact the automobile component manufacturer, which could harm the supply chain all the way up to the auto dealership. These relationships and their consequences must be fully considered in the business environment task.

Regardless of your organization's supply chain, your CISO and security stakeholders must also consider the prioritization of the company's mission, goals, stakeholders, and processes. That information must be used in the creation of roles, responsibilities, and key security decision-makers.

Administrative security controls are the policies and procedures, and their enforcement, that are essential to every organization's cybersecurity. It's a type of security control that impacts how incidents are identified.

In this governance task of the identify function, you need to understand your organization's various security policies for managing and monitoring regulatory, legal, risk, environmental, and operational requirements. This task is especially important if your organization is implementing the NIST Cybersecurity Framework after already having security policies. You will need to determine if those policies and procedures have been effective and enforceable and if they have made an impact.

Once your organization identifies your assets (which it did in a previous task), you must determine what risks they face. Keep in mind that everything has some degree of risk. You will need to determine how those risks could affect your organization's users, your business, your employees, your clients, and your critical IT systems and platforms you use in your everyday operations. What impact would particular cyber incidents have? If data is lost or stolen in a breach, how would that affect your operations, your legal standing, and your regulatory compliance? All of these risks have practical effects and associated price tags.

Now that you have taken an inventory of your organization's assets and determined all of their associated risks, it's time to manage them. Usually, you must make a compromise between usability and security. For example, implementing a lot of sophisticated methods of authentication can be good for assuring the confidentiality and integrity of your network, but your users will also need to find these authentication methods to be usable. What are the risks to your data by making these authentication methods more or less complex? What level of risk can your organization manage?

Systems that are of the greatest priority to your organization may have much less risk tolerance, while lower-priority systems may have more risk tolerance. You will need to identify how to manage risk throughout your network under the guidance of a CISO with good judgment.

Protect

The second phase of the NIST Cybersecurity Framework is *Protect*. Now that we know what we have and why it's important, we need to figure out how to develop policies and procedures to protect it all.

In NIST's words, the protect function is about how to "develop and implement the appropriate safeguards to ensure the delivery of critical infrastructure services." Each of the five functions builds upon the previous function. So now we must prepare our defenses and make sure they're effective. There are six tasks involved in the protect function.

Access control is the first task and is one of the most important tools in cybersecurity. It involves making sure that only authorized parties have access to data assets, buildings, user identities, and machine identities. There are lots of different ways to implement access control, including account credentials, cryptographic keys, and locked doors.

There are many different methodologies for implementing access control. The principle of least privilege should guide all of these methodologies. The principle of least privilege involves granting users access only to what they absolutely need in order to do their jobs, and no more. The more access is limited the more effective security can be, but a balance must be found for the sake of productivity, functionality, and usability. Some examples of these methodologies include role-based, mandatory, and discretionary access control.

Role-based access control manages access according to a user's role in the company or organization. One of the simplest ways to do this is to create user groups for each of the roles in your company's network and put individual user accounts into these groups accordingly. For instance, there could be one group for your accountants and another group for your network administrators.

Mandatory access control is a strict system in which users are unable to grant permissions to other users, even if they're the author of a file. In this methodology, access control is designed and deployed from a centralized authority.

Discretionary access control is a system that can be very flexible. For instance, a hierarchy of files may be accessed based on certain user permissions.

There are many different technologies and philosophies that can be used to implement access control according to your organization's needs. In this task, you must make sure that your organization's access control policies and procedures are effective so that only authorized parties have access to your various resources. The NIST Cybersecurity Framework considers both computerized access control and physical access control (doors, locks, security cameras) to be important, so make sure you consider both.

The human element is a major factor in cybersecurity. Many security vulnerabilities are caused by human error. Most cyberattacks involve social engineering—fooling human beings. That includes advanced persistent threats. Also, the people in your organization are the ones who must both enforce and abide by security policies. This human element makes the awareness and training task crucial. Your CISO and security stakeholders must make sure that security training programs are effective. They should also be frequent, as people learn best with some repetition and reminders. All the people in your organization, even receptionists and custodians, should have at least some security training.

The next task is to make sure that all of your organization's data is handled according to your business's risk strategy (designed in the previous identify function). We often use the confidentiality, integrity, and availability (CIA) triad of cybersecurity as a model for analyzing how cyber incidents can affect your data. To apply this triad, we must make sure that only authorized parties have access to data (confidentiality), that data isn't altered without authorization (integrity), and that data is there when needed (availability). This task involves maintaining and leveraging security policies, processes, and procedures to adequately protect critical data and the systems that support it.

While you're here, make sure your organization has incident response and business continuity procedures. Be prepared for anything. You may even need to prepare for natural disasters like hurricanes and floods.

Security is a continuous process. Check your patch management procedures. Review all of your organization's security policies periodically. You should also engage in regular security testing, which can include having a red team or performing penetration testing.

Your organization's networks implement a lot of different protective technologies. These can include, but aren't limited to, firewalls, intrusion detection and prevention systems, and thorough logging of all of your networking appliances. In this task your CISO and security stakeholders must ensure that you have policies and procedures for making sure all of these protective technologies work properly.

The combined Identify and Protect phases of the NIST Cybersecurity Framework are equivalent to the preparation phase I described earlier in the more generic incident response cycle I outlined.

Detect

The third phase of the NIST Cybersecurity Framework is *Detect*. We can't defend our organizations from what we can't see. That's what detection is all about.

Anomalies and events found in the logs of your network's multitude of devices is usually the first sign of a cyberattack. Your organization must make sure to log everything that possibly can be logged, including firewalls, antivirus, intrusion detection and intrusion prevention systems, and the behavior on all of your client and server machines. It may help if your organization has a SIEM system to feed all of these logs into, or at least some good log analysis tools. An effective SIEM will have well-designed correlation rules so that your network administrators and/or SOC analysts can get every *true positive* alert that may be useful and as few *false positive* and *false negative* alerts as possible. This may require some tweaking of your logging systems and SIEM correlation rules over time.

Anomalies and events must be detected in a timely manner, but the meaning of *timely* may be open to interpretation. Your CISO and security stakeholders will have to make decisions about that.

Your organization must make sure that you can understand the anomalies and events that occur constantly throughout your network. Not every anomaly or event is related to a cyber incident. Your employee may be interacting with a server a lot more frequently than usual because they have a special work duty, for example. Other anomalies and events are easy to overlook but may be a lot more problematic than they seem. Making sure your organization has policies and procedures to deal with these nuances is key to fulfilling this task of the detect function.

To ensure that your organization can detect security-related anomalies and events, continuous monitoring is a must. Your networks require end-to-end monitoring throughout your various IT systems. Your organization must make sure that nothing is missed.

In this task, your organization must make sure that your monitoring systems are up to the challenge. Don't just assume that your firewalls, intrusion detection and prevention, data loss prevention systems, antivirus, and logging are always working properly. Your organization must have policies and procedures in place to make sure that all of these various monitoring components have constant uptime, meaning that not only are these systems always running but also that all of the devices that should be monitored are connected to these systems effectively and as much as possible.

Physical security is also important here. Make sure the security cameras are working. Consider whether you need a human being watching the entrances and exits of your building. If a malicious entity tries to pick a lock or tailgate an employee to acquire unauthorized physical access, would they be caught?

This final task of the detect function assures that your organization has policies and procedures to make sure that your various detection processes are working as effectively and continuously as possible. Penetration testers and red teamers can be useful for making sure your organization can detect any event that may threaten your organization and your data in any way. This is how NIST defines this task: "Detection processes and procedures are maintained and tested to ensure timely and adequate awareness of anomalous events."

Not only should your detection processes undergo frequent security testing, but your organization also must delegate responsibilities properly. Make sure everyone in the organization understands their role in the detection process. Also make sure your responsiveness to detection aligns with your risk management policies and the various industry compliance regulations your organization may be subject to. Compliance can include data privacy regulations that pertain to your particular industry or jurisdiction, such the European Union's General Data Protection Regulation (GDPR).

Respond

When anomalies and events happen that may indicate cyber incidents, if we have established the first three functions of the NIST Cybersecurity Framework, we'll be able to notice them clearly and quickly. This leads to the fourth function, *Respond*, which is their equivalent to the identification or analysis phase in the generic incident response cycle. The response function has six tasks.

At this point, we have made sure that if something suspicious happens in our networks, we can see it. Now we have to do something about it. How your organization responds to a possible cyberattack can make all the difference to your cyber resilience, public reputation, and corporate bottom line. A fast, thorough, and effective response can make a huge difference when it comes to how much harm cyber attackers can do to your precious data assets and systems. Like some forms of cancer, if you catch it quickly, you may even be able to get rid of it completely. The most destructive cyberattacks are the ones that are given plenty of time to do as much damage as they possibly can. You have to make sure your organization is able to fight back ferociously and quickly.

To respond to cyber incidents effectively, the first task is to plan your incident response. Your organization should delegate a CSIRT. Then, you should sit down with your CSIRT and develop plans for addressing a variety of different types of cyber incidents. What should you do if you discover a data breach or malware that affects multiple clients, servers, and networking devices in your network? What if there are indications of an advanced persistent threat in your network? What if multiple devices in your network are hit with distributed denial-of-service (DDoS) attacks simultaneously? Your

CISO and other cybersecurity specialists should have a good idea of the different types of cyber threats your network may face. Make sure your organization designs many specific incident response procedures, and make sure you all understand what each of you is supposed to do in each situation. Think of it like doing a fire drill. These incident response procedures may be conducted during and after a cyberattack, depending on the specifics of the situation.

This task is largely the responsibility of your CISO, your legal team, and your public relations team. Depending on the nature of the incident, you may need to contact law enforcement to initiate a thorough criminal investigation. Determine whether the incident has affected your supply chain, your customers, or other stakeholders. If so, how has the incident affected them, or how may it affect them in the near future? Take all of that information and, with the help of legal and public relations specialists, determine how you should be communicating with them about the incident. Also consider your regulatory compliance responsibilities. For example, some data privacy regulations mandate that data breaches are publicly reported within a certain timeframe or else your organization could face expensive fines.

Once a cyber incident has happened, it's time to figure out why and to determine the effectiveness of your response. Which vulnerabilities were exploited? Vulnerabilities can be software bugs, hardware bugs, social engineering vulnerabilities in the form of the people who work for your organization, network configuration vulnerabilities, and vulnerabilities in your physical security. Any cyber incident likely involves the exploitation of multiple types of vulnerabilities.

Your organization may want to hire an external cybersecurity firm and/or law enforcement to perform digital forensics on the cyber incident you had. This is the task for doing that.

Now that your organization has conducted a forensic analysis of the cyber incident you faced, it's time to figure out what can be done for mitigation. Your organization should know which vulnerabilities were exploited in your networks. Mitigation can involve managing patches, developing patches, deploying patches, changing your network configuration, changing the configurations on your devices, removing malware, adding security appliances, and training the people in your organization.

The *Response* phase is the NIST Cybersecurity Framework's equivalent to a *containment, mitigation, or eradication* phase of incident response.

Recover

At this point, your organization should have lots of useful information about the cyber incident you survived. You should have a wealth of data from your forensics. Now is the time to go beyond the mitigation you did in the previous task to see how your security policies and procedures can be improved. Maybe you need better detection systems. Maybe your building needs better physical security. Maybe your employees and contractors need more effective and more frequent training. This is your opportunity to review all of your security policies and procedures and find ways to improve them.

That means it's time for *Recover*, the final phase in the NIST Cybersecurity Framework. This is equivalent to *post-incident* or *lessons learned* in other frameworks.

So, a cyber incident happened. Unfortunately, they can't all be prevented. But your organization orchestrated an effective incident response. You've delegated a CSIRT consisting of staff from your IT department, legal department, public relations, and CISO. You prepared thorough incident response plans. You let everyone in your CSIRT understand what their roles and responsibilities are. You got law enforcement and digital forensics specialists to work as required. You communicated to parties who needed to be informed about the cyber incident. You did your best to mitigate the vulnerabilities that the cyber attacker exploited, and you checked to see if any of your security policies and procedures could be improved. Now it's time to recover from the cyber incident. This final function has three tasks. They're similar to three of the tasks in the respond function but should be conducted from a different perspective.

Just as your organization should have incident response plans prior to a cyber incident occurring, you should also have incident recovery plans. Your incident recovery plans can also be designed by your CSIRT under the direction of your CISO.

Different types of cyber incidents will need different forms of recovery. Whether your network is on your premises, on the cloud, or a hybrid, as much of your data as possible should be backed up. Preferably, there should be multiple backups in different locations. Backups can help your organization to recover from a wide range of incidents from natural disasters to ransomware attacks to data loss from theft. Institutions like hospitals and schools are the primary targets of ransomware these days. Occasionally, organizations with thorough backups have still paid ransoms in ransomware incidents because they couldn't recover from their backups quickly enough to avoid interrupting their essential operations. When your organization engages in recovery planning, you should consider how long it would take to recover from your backups and test your backup recovery just in case.

Backing up your data in multiple physical locations, including in the cloud, is key in case a cyber incident occurs at one of those backup locations. That leaves you with other backups for the sake of useful redundancy.

You should also plan for business continuity in the event of natural disasters and similar phenomenon. Many large organizations have backup *hot sites* that can act as new work sites almost immediately if something bad happens to their usual work site, or *cold sites* that can act as new work sites with some preparation. Your incident recovery and business continuity plans will differ according to the unique needs of your organization.

Whether your networks are on premises or in the cloud, you will also need some redundant network capacity in the form of extra servers, extra bandwidth, more firewalls, more routers, and so on. This can be useful if a lot of your network goes out of service due to cyberattack. Acquiring this sort of redundancy is much easier if at least some of your network is on the cloud because then your organization won't have to buy the extra equipment and space directly; you could just call your cloud provider.

In the respond function, we looked for ways that your organization could improve your policies and procedures with the information you learned from a cyber incident. Here, in the recover function, is your chance to do this again, focusing on your recovery plans this time.

Did your organization back up the data that you needed to recover from? Was the backup process efficient and successful? Were you able to get your network's crucial services back online quickly? Were there any interruptions to your organization's everyday operations? Did your business have continuity if a work site or a large part of your network was periodically disabled? Figure out what went right and what went wrong. Make improvements to your organization's recovery plans based on that knowledge.

Here's the final task of the final function. In the response function, you decided how you would communicate information about the cyber incident to your organization's stakeholders. Now it's time to make similar decisions about your recovery operation. It's time to communicate recovery plans and processes with internal managers and the executive team. This sharing of knowledge will make your organization more resilient in the face of future cyber incidents.

ISO 27000 Cybersecurity Frameworks

The International Organization for Standardization (ISO) is an international standards body that pertains to all areas of industrialization. The ISO 27000 has a series of cybersecurity frameworks with a few similar concepts to the NIST Cybersecurity Framework, but it's a completely different way to approach incident response.

The ISO 27000 frameworks consist of the following:

- **ISO 27001:** The specification for an information security management system (ISMS), a set of policies and procedures for systematically managing an organization's sensitive data.

- **ISO 27002:** Defines information security control mechanisms that could be anything from physical controls like doors, to technical controls like antivirus software, to administrative controls such as security policies. This standard is designed to address the specific security requirements identified through formal risk assessment.
- **ISO 27003:** Provides help and guidance in implementing an ISMS.
- **ISO 27004:** Pertains to ISMS measurement and metrics that can be applied to the security controls defined in ISO 27002.
- **ISO 27005:** Provides more detail on security risk management.
- **ISO 27006:** Provides guidelines for the accreditation of organizations offering ISMS certification.

If you work in a CSIRT, the most relevant information should be in ISO 27001, which features the *plan, do, check*, and *act* (PDCA) cycle, its equivalent to an incident response cycle.

Plan involves creating ISMS policy, objectives, processes, and procedures related to risk management and the improvement of information security to meet your organization's objectives. This is the equivalent to a *preparation* phase.

Do applies to the implementation of ISMS policy, controls, processes, and procedures. This is equivalent to a *containment, mitigation, or eradication* phase.

Check involves monitoring and reviewing the ISMS. This phase assesses and measures the performance of the processes against the ISMS policy, objectives, and practical experience. It's similar to a *recovery* phase.

Act combines parts of a *recovery* phase with a *post-incident* phase. It involves updating and improving the ISMS, engaging in preventative actions after the results of the ISMS internal audit is complete, and improving your incident response accordingly.

CIS Controls

The Center for Internet Security (CIS) is a private nonprofit organization that was founded in October 2000. It has its own cybersecurity framework that was designed to be compatible with the NIST Cybersecurity Framework.

Their framework involves 20 controls. Here's a brief explanation of what they are:

1. **Inventory and Control of Hardware Assets:** Inventory and track all of your devices on your network so that authorized devices are given access, and unauthorized and unmanaged devices are prevented from gaining access.
2. **Inventory and Control of Software Assets:** Inventory and track all of your software in your network only, so authorized software is installed and can execute, and unauthorized and unmanaged software is found and prevented from installation or execution. This is similar to the first control but addresses software instead of hardware.
3. **Continuous Vulnerability Management:** This control is about being aware of new security vulnerabilities, watching for them in your network in the many forms they can take, and patching and mitigating them as much as possible.
4. **Controlled Use of Administrative Privileges:** Administrative privileges in a network are the most destructive if they fall into the hands of a hostile entity. This control tracks and monitors the use of administrative privileges to make sure they're used appropriately and carefully.
5. **Secure Configuration for Hardware and Software on Mobile Devices, Laptops, Workstations, and Servers:** Create, implement, and manage the security configuration of all devices in your network using a rigorous configuration management and change control process to prevent attackers from exploiting vulnerable services and settings.
6. **Maintenance, Monitoring, and Analysis of Audit Logs:** Every device that can be logged should be logged, as much as possible. The information the logs provide can help your organization recover from and prevent cyber incidents.
7. **Email and Web Browser Protections:** Reduce opportunities for cyberattackers to manipulate human behavior through email and web browsers.

8. **Malware Defenses:** Control and prevent malware through multiple points in the enterprise, while optimizing the use of automation to record malicious activity and prevent malware execution.
9. **Limitation and Control of Network Ports, Protocols, and Services:** There are thousands of internet ports under the TCP/IP system. Monitor, control, and limit internet ports to minimize windows of vulnerability available to attackers.
10. **Data Recovery Capability:** Back up as much data as you can, and make sure you can effectively recover from your backups when it's necessary.
11. **Secure Configuration for Network Devices, such as Firewalls, Routers, and Switches:** Create and thoroughly manage the security configuration of network infrastructure devices using a rigorous configuration management and change control process in order to prevent attackers from exploiting vulnerable services and settings.
12. **Boundary Defense:** Detect, prevent, and monitor data transferring to networks of different trust levels with a focus on more sensitive data.
13. **Data Protection:** These are the processes and tools used to prevent data exfiltration, mitigate the effects of exfiltrated data, and ensure the privacy and integrity of sensitive information.
14. **Controlled Access Based on the Need to Know:** This is similar to the principle of least privilege. Users should have access only to data they absolutely must have in order to do their jobs. This security control limits data access accordingly.
15. **Wireless Access Control:** These are the processes and tools used to manage the security of wireless networks and wireless client systems.
16. **Account Monitoring and Control:** Actively manage the life cycle of system and application accounts in order to minimize opportunities for cyberattackers to exploit them.
17. **Implement a Security Awareness and Training Program:** This should be given to every single person who works in your organization, especially roles that are "mission critical to the

business and its security." Identify the specific knowledge, skills, and abilities needed to support defense of the enterprise; develop and execute an integrated plan to assess, identify gaps, and remediate through policy, organizational planning, training, and awareness programs.

18. **Application Software Security:** Manage the security life cycle of all in-house developed and acquired software in order to prevent, detect, and correct security weaknesses.
19. **Incident Response and Management:** Protect the organization's information, as well as its reputation, by developing and implementing an incident response infrastructure for quickly discovering an attack and then effectively containing the damage, eradicating the attacker's presence, and restoring the integrity of the network and systems. Using the NIST Cybersecurity Framework can complement this control.
20. **Penetration Tests and Red Team Exercises:** This is all about simulating cyberattacks to find security vulnerabilities that should be removed, patched, or mitigated accordingly.

CIS has a guide to mapping its CIS Controls to the NIST Cybersecurity Framework that you can download as an Excel spreadsheet: `https://www.cisecurity.org/white-papers/cis-controls-v7-1-mapping-to-nist-csf/`.

COBIT Cybersecurity Framework

The Control Objectives for Information and Related Technology (COBIT) standard was created by Information Systems Audit and Control Association (ISACA), a popular cybersecurity standards and certification body. The latest standard as of this writing is COBIT 2019.

COBIT is designed to be used with the NIST Cybersecurity Framework, or on its own, according to your organization's needs. It consists of these domains:

- Planning and Organization
- Delivering and Support

- Acquiring and Implementation
- Monitoring and Evaluating

There's limited information about the details of the COBIT 2019 standard online because ISACA encourages people in the business community to pay for access. It does offer a COBIT 2019 certification that could be useful for your CSIRT members. It also has guides to implementing COBIT 2019 with other security frameworks. If you'd like to learn more about COBIT, it's best to visit ISACA's COBIT web resources at `https://www.isaca.org/resources/cobit`.

Security Frameworks and Cloud Security

Security frameworks can be helpful when it comes to designing and implementing your organization's incident response policies and procedures. But security frameworks aren't perfect. It's helpful to understand some of the constructive criticism people in the cybersecurity community have about them. It'll help you better refine your incident response with greater objectivity and perspective.

One noted lack is that the NIST Cybersecurity Framework may be insufficient for protecting cloud networks. The use of cloud providers has really grown in the past decade or so. AWS is probably the most popular cloud provider for the enterprise. Other tech giants have their own competing platforms, such as Google Cloud Platform and Microsoft Azure.

The cloud is useful for many businesses. You can greatly expand your network capacity without having to buy more of your own servers and the space for them in your facilities. Cloud networks are scalable. Maybe one day you'll realize that your organization needs double the number of servers. All you have to do is contact your cloud provider and pay for it. Maybe the following year, you'll find you'll need only half as many servers as before. You can just contact your provider and pay for less capacity and bandwidth. It's a lot more work to adjust the size of your network if you have to maintain your own servers and datacenters.

Given the popularity and growth of cloud networks, it's important to understand how the NIST Cybersecurity Framework might not be enough to manage their unique security needs.

The NIST Cybersecurity Framework says log files should be kept for 30 days. Data breaches often take longer than a month to discover and respond to, so the log retention standard should probably be a few months or more.

The NIST Cybersecurity Framework lacks clarity on who's responsible for security in the cloud. No matter which cloud provider you use, the rule is that cloud infrastructure is the responsibility of the cloud provider (such as AWS), whereas your data and applications in the cloud are the responsibility of your organization. For example, AWS has to make sure that only authorized parties have physical access to their cloud servers. Your responsibility is to patch software vulnerabilities and use the software security controls your cloud provider offers you.

The NIST encourages the principle of least privilege. Each user should have access only to data and resources that they need to do their jobs and no more, but the NIST Cybersecurity Framework doesn't define tenant delegation, or virtual tenants. Virtual tenants are the entities that share resources within a cloud provider. Assigning virtual tenancy keeps a cloud customer's administrators from interfering with other virtual tenants.

Without proper tenant delegation in the cloud, managing sensitive data between tenants can be risky. One tenant has no right to access another tenant's data, but without defining which data belongs to which entity, this area can get murky when it comes to security control configuration.

Nonetheless security frameworks are useful for many organizations to design their incident response plans, policies, and procedures. But whether or not you implement frameworks, you must have a well-designed incident response and delegate a CSIRT.

Chapter 6
Step 6: Control Your Data Assets

Ultimately, cybersecurity is all about protecting data. It's true that your organization's hardware, such as PCs, mobile devices, servers, peripherals, and networking appliances, are expensive and have monetary value, especially when they're new. However, data is arguably more valuable and should be the main focus of your cybersecurity efforts. All that fancy equipment is purposeless without data.

As I've mentioned previously, cyber threats to your company's data can have many detrimental effects to your business. If your online store is offline, customers can't buy your products (especially in a pandemic, when brick-and-mortar stores may be closed). I mentioned in step 3 that data breaches are probably much more common than you'd think from news coverage, and according to IBM's Cost of a Data Breach Study 2020, the average cost of a data breach in the United States is $8.64 million. If your company doesn't work in retail, you still need your computer network to be running to conduct your everyday business. You likely also have some sensitive data—financial data such as credit cards and bank accounts, and perhaps even research and development. We address the reasons why cybersecurity is extremely important to your business regardless of its size, industry, or geographic location throughout this book.

In step 6, I'll explain in greater detail how to protect your data. Even if your background is in business and you aren't a computer nerd, it's important for you to understand some of this stuff. It'll help you understand how to develop a strong security team and how to determine whether they're working effectively.

The CIA Triad

I aim to mention the CIA triad in every single cybersecurity-related book I'll ever write. The concept is *that* important to understanding cybersecurity as a whole. I already mentioned it briefly in step 3, but let's explore the concept further.

Remember that the CIA in the CIA triad stands for confidentiality, integrity, and availability. All cyber threats impact *at least one* of these components, and many threats impact two or three components at the same time.

Confidentiality involves keeping data accessible only to authorized parties. It's the main reason why we encrypt data. You should be able to decrypt your own data and other data that you have permission to see. Even if you know nothing about cryptography, software applications such as your web browser and email client are designed to handle the encryption and decryption for you. Data breaches are probably the worst threat to data confidentiality out there, as I have explained. Data in the hands of those who aren't allowed to have it can result in serious repercussions.

Integrity involves making sure that only authorized parties can alter or delete data. If cybercriminals put malware into your Word and Excel documents (something that does happen), that's an integrity threat. Another integrity threat is vandalizing a website, such as if a threat actor made a company's home page say something like, "The CEO sucks!"

A frequent and harmful sort of cyberattack occurs when Domain Name System (DNS) records are poisoned. DNS technology is what makes it possible to visit Wiley's website using `https://wiley.com`, rather than having to type 63.97.118.67 in your web browser address bar. DNS is used for all internet services that use domain names, not only websites, meaning email and file transfer protocol (FTP), among many others. Even us cyber geeks rely upon domain names instead of depending on memorizing IP addresses. And when IPv6 addresses become more common, we'll be even more grateful for domain names so we don't have to memorize addresses like 2001:0db8:0001:0000:0000:0ab9:C0A8:0102.

Anyway, one of the main reasons why cybercriminals poison DNS records is so users will visit a malicious website with malware or phishing, rather than the legitimate website a domain name is supposed to point to. We don't even type domain names out that often these days. But our web browsers remember which sites we visit, and we also use search engines to find websites. My web browser remembers that I visit `https://killstar.com` quite frequently, but it probably doesn't remember Killstar's IP addresses. This means that if a threat actor poisons my DNS server to associate the domain name with a malicious website, it will effectively attack my PC and phone. DNS poisoning is a great example of a cyber threat to integrity.

The last component of the CIA triad is availability. Availability involves making sure data is there when you need it. If a distributed denial-of-service attack knocks your internet servers offline, that's a classic threat to availability. Another availability threat involves physically destroying your hard drives without your consent. One has a temporary effect, one is permanent (unless all of your data is backed up elsewhere), but they impact availability all the same.

Cyberattacks are getting increasingly sophisticated, so ransomware that targets the enterprise is now threatening to breach data, not just maliciously encrypt it. In these cases, the entire CIA triad is impacted. Another example of cyber threats that impact the entirety of the CIA triad is the rise of modular malware, in which cyberattckers send multiple modules to victim machines. The attacker orchestrates everything through their command-and-control server. First, they infect a target machine and maintain persistence, which means you can't easily stop it or get rid of it, threatening your integrity if it alters the data on your computer. Then they send modules to the infected machine, and each module can cause different problems. The spyware module threatens your confidentiality because it's used to spy on a victim's data and computer activities. A ransomware module threatens availability. And they keep sending malware to their victim's computers, finding multiple ways to profit from harming them. Financial gain drives the large majority of cyber threats.

Access Control

Access control as it pertains to cybersecurity is all about controlling access to your data: determining the files or other data resources that should be accessible and who can access them. A good access control system permits access only when necessary. A concept to keep in mind is the principle of least privilege. People should have access only to the data and computer systems they need in order to do their jobs and absolutely no more. By limiting access to your data, you reduce its cyberattack surface. You protect your data by making sure it's exposed and used only as is absolutely necessary to reduce the risk of something bad happening to it.

There are many different ways to implement access control. All effective ways of implementing access control stick to the principle of least privilege and also assure accountability—to make sure anything your workers do with your data is logged and traceable to them specifically. For that reason, your employees should never share their user accounts with anyone else, even if they have the same role in your organization. Being able to trace all actions on your data to a specific human being will help tremendously with both investigating cyber incidents and auditing by third parties. Proper authorship helps your incident response team, and it helps to ensure regulatory compliance.

Here are some of the more commonly used access control systems. Determining which are right for your organization depends on how your company operates and what type of data is being accessed. A strong security team and knowledgeable computer networking professionals can help you decide which access control systems are best for your needs.

- With discretionary access control (DAC), the owner of the data, such as the author of a file, decides who has access to it.
- Mandatory access control (MAC) is a very strict system. In a MAC system, users are granted access rights based on security clearances. In other words, access rights are assigned based on regulations from a central authority. This isn't a practical access control system, so it should be used only for the most sensitive types of data.
- Role-based access control (RBAC), as the name implies, is based on the role a user has in your organization. Users with the same role, such as accountants or system administrators, can be put into user groups and then permissions are assigned to those user groups.
- Attribute-based access control (ABAC) is complicated, but it can be useful. In ABAC, permissions are granted according to a series of attributes, such as a user's role, what time of day it is, where the user is, and which functionality the user needs. It's a highly customizable system, but it can be complicated to administer.

Patch Management

Proper patch management is essential to protecting your data and keeping your operating systems and applications secure. When software developers discover new vulnerabilities, they work to develop and deploy patches to fix those vulnerabilities.

If you've ever used Windows 10, you've likely noticed that sometimes the operating system doesn't allow you to shut down your computer right away. About once a week you'll see a message telling you not to turn off your computer because it's running updates. In these situations, Microsoft has sent new security updates (what patches are often called) to your computer, and Windows uses the shutdown process to install them.

If you use an iPhone or an Android phone, every so often you need to accept a new security update. Your phone will reboot and take a few minutes to install and configure the patches before you can use it again.

All popular operating systems have frequent security patches. The same applies to your apps and other software programs you use within those operating systems. Keeping software secure is complicated and a lot of hard work. Before internet use was common, security patches were often installed off of floppy disks and CD-ROMs. Those older PCs of the 1980s to mid-1990s were also patched less frequently because they usually weren't connected to the internet. The internet introduced a massive new means for cyberattacking our computers, but that same internet makes deploying patches a lot easier.

Occasionally, a patch or update may make your computer less secure. For the vulnerabilities it mitigated, it may have introduced even worse vulnerabilities to your software. When these new vulnerabilities are discovered, a new patch will be necessary, and it's the responsibility of the software developer to create and deploy it. The vast majority of the time, your computers, servers, and mobile devices are the most secure when they've installed their most recent updates.

Your organization needs to make sure that your operating systems, applications, and networking devices such as firewalls and routers are configured to automatically install their latest updates. Firewalls and antivirus software need frequent patches so they can prevent or mitigate newly discovered cyber threats. Sometimes they can be patched while in operation, whereas other times they may need to be rebooted in order to install patches. Your security team needs to decide what sort of patch management works best for your organization. For instance, perhaps patches that require rebooting to be installed can be configured to install only during times your employees aren't using those computers. This can get more complicated if your company has servers on your premises. You may need to design your patch management so that some servers keep running while other servers reboot to install patches, and then have the newly patched servers operate while the other servers are patched. Effective patch management is essential when it comes to protecting your organization's precious data assets.

Physical Security and Your Data

Physical security is an often overlooked factor when it comes to protecting and controlling your organization's data. But your organization must be vigilant about it in order to protect your precious data. No one should have physical access to your computers unless they're authorized to. Additionally, there are a few physical security risks your security team should be prepared for.

Tailgating is when an unauthorized person follows an authorized person (such as an employee or contractor) into the building, bypassing any physical locks, receptionists, and security guards. A tailgater will exploit your employee's authorization to pass through these security controls in order to acquire unauthorized access. They could even tailgate right into your server room. There are specific solutions for preventing tailgating, such as specially designed anti-tailgating doors.

Document theft is another physical security risk. You could have sensitive information printed on paper or saved to USB drives or other media. If a permitted visitor or an intruder can see these documents or removable data media, they could pocket them and stealthily slip them out of the workplace.

Malicious parties also sometimes steal employee ID cards, lanyards, and key fobs in order to gain unauthorized physical access. Train your employees to use these authentication devices carefully. Make sure they always know where they are so they aren't stolen.

Security cameras, security guards, and receptionists can be useful physical security controls. People should be watching all of the ways a person can enter your building so they can prevent unauthorized access. Doors and physical locks are also important to use properly.

No one should be able to touch your organization's computers or access other ways data is physically handled (printed documents, USB drives, mobile devices, DVDs, removable external disk drives, SD cards) without authorization. This is a key factor in controlling your organization's data.

Malware

Malware is one of the most common threats to data. I mentioned malware in multiple parts of this book. Now it's time to explain the basics of malware.

Laypeople often call all malware viruses when, in fact, a computer virus is simply a type of malware. All computer viruses are malware, but not all malware are viruses, in the same way that all bananas are fruit, but not all fruits are bananas.

Malware is all software that is designed to cause harm. The word comes from the term *malicious software*. However, categorizing something as malware can be subjective.

A media player that was popular in the 1990s was considered malware because although it did legitimately play audio and video, it spied on user activity. I consider the application to be both a Trojan and spyware, but some people may disagree. The application's developer, and especially their lawyers, would definitely disagree.

Another example of malware is a cryptominer, which uses a computer's CPU and memory to generate cryptocurrency. If a cryptominer is used with the consent of the computer's owner, then it isn't malware, but if it's used without consent, then it definitely is malware. In fact, some of the cryptominers that are used legitimately are also often used maliciously.

There are several general types of malware. Viruses and worms are named based on how the malware travels from one computer to another. A virus propagates by inserting a copy of itself into and becoming part of another file or application. It always changes the data on an infected computer. A worm replicates functional copies of itself without altering files or application on your computer. It simply sends copies of itself through a security vulnerability.

Ransomware maliciously encrypts your data without giving you the decryption key. It will display a ransom note as a text file, on a local web page, or in some other obvious way, usually demanding cryptocurrency in exchange for getting your files back. It used to primarily target consumers, but enterprises can pay much more money (individually) for ransoms, so they've become the primary ransomware target in recent years. Organizations are now much better at backing up their data, so now some of the latest ransomware attacks threaten to breach their victims' data as well.

Bot malware infects machines to do a botnet's bidding. Any kind of computer or mobile device can be infected with a bot, especially if it uses the internet. A botnet can consist of more than thousands of malware-infected machines. Cybercriminals control their actions through a command-and-control server. Some of the most frequent uses of botnets include DDS attacks and the spread of modular malware.

A DDS attack uses a lot of computers to overwhelm a network target with data until it can't handle it anymore, forcing the network target to go offline, out of service. Modular malware has many different modular components. After initial infection and the maintenance of persistence, modules can be sent to an infected machine to do multiple types of bad things. (*Bad things* is the technical term, of course.) Modular malware first became common on Android phones and tablets, but now all popular operating systems, including Windows, are targeted by modular malware. An infected machine may be hit with a cryptominer, then spyware, then ransomware, and so on, all while the threat actor tries to find different ways to harm their target for profit. These modules could be sent to an infected machine over the course of days, weeks, or even months.

A Trojan infects a targeted machine by pretending to be something the user wants. They're named after the Trojan horses of Greek myth. A Trojan can be anything from a malicious email attachment in the form of an image or document to that malicious media player from the 1990s I mentioned to a deliberately malware-infected website. The common thread is that Trojans require user interaction in order to be executed on a targeted machine. I may unintentionally allow malware on my computer if I can be fooled into thinking it's a fun game, an Excel spreadsheet I need, or a cute meme with cats in it. That's how Trojans work. The majority of Android and iPhone malware are Trojans: useful or fun mobile apps that accidentally end up in the Google Play Store or Apple App Store. Google's approach to preventing malware in their store is to permit apps to be uploaded to their store by default and also to scan them for malware before they become available in the store. Apple's approach is to only whitelist (permit) apps in their store after they've passed an approval process. Either way, when Google and Apple discover an app in their stores is malware, they remove it and usually blacklist (forbid) the developer from using their store ever again, especially if malware was uploaded to their store deliberately. Malware has been found in the Google Play Store more frequently than in the App Store. But don't get overconfident, iPhone users. Malware has ended up in the App Store too, multiple times.

Spyware is exactly what it sounds like. It's malware that spies on its victims. Spyware could be sharing the data on your computer without your consent, or it could be monitoring what you do with your computer. Or it could be doing both.

One subcategory of spyware, called a *keylogger*, logs the keys you type into your computer. Originally, keyloggers were mainly hardware, a device that's plugged in between your keyboard and your PC. These days, keyloggers are mainly malware. Recent keylogger malware not only tells a cyberattacker what you type, but some keyloggers also share your web browser cookies and history, login credentials for social media and various online services, application settings, and perhaps other activity logs on your computer, such as when you boot your operating system or when you launch certain applications.

Stalkerware is another type of spyware primarily used by abusive romantic partners or ex-partners to spy on their victims. The applications that are used as stalkerware are often marketed as handy tools to monitor children or employees, but an abusive partner could use stalkerware to see their target's texting activity, such as whom and what they've been texting, social media activity that isn't publicly available, emails, and even where their targets are through GPS geolocation.

There are lots of other types of malware, but those are the most common categories. Malware usually belongs to more than one category, even if it isn't modular. Spyware can be a virus, ransomware can be a worm, and malicious cryptominers can be Trojans.

I strongly believe that all PCs, servers, and mobile devices should have antivirus software, regardless of its operating system. Any computer that can receive data from an external source can become infected by malware, whether through the internet or some other network, or through removable devices like DVDs, USB drives, or SD cards. Antivirus software is imperfect, making it impossible for antivirus software to detect 100 percent of all malware. There are lots of different ways that malware can be detected, such as through signatures or heuristics, but the technological complexity of those methods of detecting malware is beyond the scope of this book. What you should know is that frequently updated antivirus software makes your computer much better protected from malware than it would be without. It's kind of like seatbelts, airbags, and safe driving. There's no guarantee you won't have a car accident, but you'll be less likely to be harmed in a car accident.

I'm frequently asked to identify the best antivirus software. I used to work for a few antivirus developers, but still, the answer to that question isn't a simple one. Some antivirus software is better at detecting some types of malware and not as good as detecting other types of malware. The effectiveness of antivirus software can change a lot depending on its most recent updates. For the sake of your business, I recommend visiting AV-Test's website (`www.av-test.org`) and reading the latest ratings for antivirus software for the operating systems you use.

Cryptography Basics

The concept of cryptography has come up a few times, but here, we will explore the topic in more depth. Cryptography is the art of scrambling information into unreadable gibberish for the sake of confidentiality. The application of cryptography is encryption.

Earlier in this book, I mentioned the numbers station phenomenon. Those are shortwave radio stations that transmit series of numbers that mean nothing at all to people who don't have a one-time pad to decrypt the messages. That's one example of analog cryptography—cryptography without the use of computers.

Hundreds of years before computers were invented, there were other forms of analog cryptography. Ancient civilizations would use a cryptographic code to communicate war tactics to their soldiers. A physical device, such as a scytale, would be used to decrypt those messages. Leaders might want to give their soldiers a message that includes the location and time of a strike, but they would not want the opposing force to be able to understand the message if they intercepted it.

Mechanical cryptography was a major factor in World War II. The Nazis encrypted their messages with their mechanical Enigma machine. Alan Turing, the father of modern computing, worked in the United Kingdom's Bletchley Park, engaged in cracking Nazi encryption for the benefit of the Allied forces. Enigma machines looked like antiquated mechanical keyboards in wooden boxes with electrical wires. Cracking Enigma's cipher was a tremendous effort for Turing's mathematical brilliance, but he wasn't alone. In Bletchley Park, Turing collaborated with Gordon Welchman and had a lot of help from Polish mathematicians. But the Nazis caught onto how the Allies were cracking their codes, and they kept working to make their ciphers more complex as the war went on. It was a cat-and-mouse game of cipher cracking and better cipher deployment, similar to what we see today with digital cryptography.

So, how does encryption work on our computers and on the internet? First, we start with unencrypted data, called *cleartext* or *plaintext*. Digitally, we use symmetric key cryptography and asymmetric key cryptography to turn the cleartext into encrypted data called *ciphertext*.

With symmetric key cryptography, the code that's used to encrypt data can be reversed to decrypt it. For instance, if the code is X + 30 × 10 / 3 = Y, then Y × 3 / 10 – 30 = X can decrypt it. Both the sender and the recipient need to keep their keys secret for it to be secure. If a cyberattacker acquires either key, they'll be able to access the data.

Asymmetric key cryptography is a lot more complex in its ciphers because asymmetrically encrypted data can't be decrypted by reversing the encryption key. An attacker would need the specific decryption key in order to decrypt the data. For that reason, asymmetric key encryption is used for public key cryptography—the way computers on the internet send their keys to you.

Furthermore, encryption technologies can be stream ciphers, meaning they can be used for data in transit, such as through the internet. They can also be block ciphers, the kind of cryptography used to encrypt the data in storage on your hard drive.

Hypertext Transfer Protocol Secure (HTTPS) is one of the most common ways we use encryption every day, although you may not be aware of it. The internet protocol uses Transport Layer Security (TLS) encryption to encrypt web data traveling between your phone or PC and the web server. Google, Apple, Mozilla, and other major tech companies have made it a priority in recent years to encourage as much HTTPS use as possible, as opposed to the unencrypted HTTP. For example, web browsers will give you a big bold warning if you try to visit HTTP sites, and Google prioritizes HTTPS websites in its search results.

Some of the other types of encryption you may have heard of are Advanced Encryption Standard (AES), Pretty Good Privacy (PGP), and Rivest–Shamir–Adleman (RSA). There are thousands of different cryptographic technologies, each of which may be more appropriate for one function than another.

All cryptographic ciphers will eventually be cracked, as more powerful computers fall into the hands of cybercriminals. Much like the activities between Bletchley Park and the Nazis, there's a constant battle between cryptography developers and crackers. Older, weaker forms of encryption must always be replaced with newer stronger forms of encryption.

In my years of reporting cyberattacks in the media, I found that attackers evade encryption through implementation vulnerabilities a lot more frequently than they do by cracking the encryption itself. For example, the super strong lock on my door is pointless if I keep my key under my doormat where a burglar can find it.

Some implementation vulnerabilities can be alarming. Let me tell you about Heartbleed, a vulnerability in a library that was used in a multitude of TLS implementations. It was discovered in 2014 and patched quickly after, but it existed in a lot of TLS use for about two-and-a-half years before it was discovered. It affected Android phones and many online services such as GitHub, Stripe payment platform, the Canada Revenue Agency, Ars Technica, and Amazon Web Services, among others.

The Heartbleed vulnerability was caused by a simple syntax error. If you're not a computer programmer, that means a character like { or [was forgotten or put in the wrong place. eWEEK estimated that at least $500 million was collectively lost through this vulnerability.

There's a new threat to cryptography everywhere. Quantum computers have been in development for many years now, and they could be used in production in the next few years. Without getting too technical, because of the difference between quantum computers and binary computers, quantum computers will be able to crack all kinds of binary encryption in no time, rendering it pointless. All the computers the world has ever used and is currently using now are binary, and all of our digital encryption is binary. Quantum computing presents a lot of promise, but quantum computers could also be very harmful in the hands of cybercriminals. IBM and the National Institute for Standards and Technology (NIST) have been working on the development of quantum-safe cryptography for years. Pretty soon, we will need to make sure that all of the cryptography we use is quantum safe.

It should be common wisdom now that as much of our data as possible should be encrypted, preferably 100 percent of it. Cryptography is built into many of the products and services your IT team is interested in procuring for your business. A strong security team can help your business choose the many kinds of cryptography you need to protect your precious data assets. And then they can make sure that it's implemented as effectively as possible—no figurative door keys under doormats.

Bring Your Own Device and Working from Home

Modern computer networks have two challenges you'll need to address, bring-your-own-device (BYOD) policies and working from home.

BYOD involves permitting devices into your network that your workers own and that your IT department doesn't manage. One of the most common examples is an employee connecting their personal phone to the office WiFi. It's often necessary to permit BYOD for the sake of productivity and functionality, but it introduces new security threats to your organization's data. For instance, your employee's phone could introduce malware into your network. Or they could put Excel spreadsheets of company financial data onto their own USB thumb drive and take it home from them.

If your business must permit BYOD, you must have a policy to manage it and to mitigate its associated risks. An example could be something like this:

- "All employee-owned phones, laptops, and USB drives must be scanned by our antivirus before they can be mounted into the company network."
- "Employees are forbidden to transfer files from networked folders onto their own devices."
- "Only x, y, and z type devices are permitted to connect to our network, not a, b, and c type devices."

These policies aren't explained only to employees, but they can also be built into the systems that your administrators use to manage your network. Some companies even offer BYOD management solutions, such as the IBM Security MaaS360 BYOD Solution.

Sit down with your security team and decide if BYOD is necessary in the first place. If it is, work on how you'll manage it through policies and perhaps specially designed vendor solutions.

Then there's the increasing work-from-home (WFH) situation, accelerated by the Covid-19 pandemic. For businesses to function, you often need to permit your workers to WFH either sometimes or all of the time. Remote workers will connect to your organization's internal network through the internet. This poses similar risks to BYOD—introducing malware and other possible cyberattacks and also introducing the possibility of your company's sensitive data being exposed through devices you don't own or manage.

Your business should offer a virtual private network (VPN) service for your remote workers if they need to connect to your internal network, as opposed to just submitting their work through email or web applications without additional company-managed encryption. There are many commercial VPNs such as ExpressVPN and NordVPN, but those are better for consumer use. Your security team can use OpenVPN or similar software to set up and administrate your own VPN servers. When implemented properly, it will encrypt their connection from home, through the internet, to your organization's internal network. But security isn't the only consideration here; you also need to consider functionality. Recently I had to use the VPN servers of one of the companies I work for. It was frustrating to use because they didn't allocate enough bandwidth or capacity to it, so my connection was considerably slower than when I didn't use it. That's not OpenVPN's fault. If you set up OpenVPN with enough capacity and bandwidth, it shouldn't be noticeably slower than any network connection without a VPN. Get your computer networking specialists to make sure your own VPN servers work well for your employees. That way, they won't be discouraged from using it, and it won't hurt their productivity. Some employees and contractors may also need help from your IT department to set up a VPN connection on their PC, MacBook, or phone.

Data Loss Prevention

Data loss prevention systems are information technology solutions that are designed to monitor the use of data in your corporate network to assure that sensitive or critical information doesn't leave it.

Vendors that sell data loss prevention (DLP) systems use the terms *data leak* and *data loss*. People often confuse the terms, but they mean different things.

A data leak occurs when sensitive data is exposed outside of your network, while your network still has the data. In a simple data leak incident, sensitive data in your company's network is just copied onto a machine or device outside of your network. This is still bad because you must keep sensitive data confidential, but at least your company still has its own copy of the data. In DLP language, data leaks are a threat that's exclusive to the confidentiality component of the CIA triad.

In this context, data loss means not only that your sensitive data was breached to outside of your network, but your network actually lost the data. For example, a credit card number that your company is supposed to retain was not just exposed to cybercriminals, but also your company no longer has the credit card number. Data leaks are bad, but data loss is even worse. Data loss is a threat to the confidentiality component of the CIA triad and also to the availability component, and possibly to the integrity component too. It's a toxic triple threat.

There are three different levels of technology that an organization can deploy to prevent data leaks and data loss. The standard measures are the first-level security controls that all companies must have in their networks. Firewalls can be configured to protect your data by blocking TCP/IP network ports and by making sure applications can manage data only in designated ways. Intrusion detection systems monitor your network for unauthorized access, making sure that external intrusion cannot penetrate your network without being noticed by your security team. Antivirus software can prevent malware from entering your network, and malware is often used to exfiltrate data. These technologies are the least your network should have in order to protect your cybersecurity, but they must be configured and deployed with care.

Advanced measures are the second level, and they go a step further by implementing artificial intelligence (AI) and machine learning. Machine learning uses AI to modify how it detects abnormal network and application behavior. It's supposed to improve over time with use, so in a sense, the machine "learns." Temporal reasoning algorithms can detect abnormal access to data. One way is by deploying honeypots, computers put in your network that are designed to attract cyberattacks to them. A modern honeypot has two purposes. The first is to prevent cyberattacks from targeting your more valuable machines (when it comes to managing your data and the functioning of your network), and the other is to record how cyberattacks behave so your AI systems and security team can learn how to prevent them.

The third level of technology involves designed systems. This is the technology that's specifically sold as DLP systems. They detect and prevent unauthorized attempts to copy or send sensitive data, whether intentional or unintentional.

Your company can choose the first level, the first and second levels, or all three levels when it comes to preventing data loss and data leaks to your network. When a vendor sells a DLP solution, they are referring to the third level. Your security team can help you choose how to implement data loss prevention in the most effective way according to the specific needs of your business. If you just have a small network, the first level of standard measures may be sufficient.

Managed Service Providers

In a general sense, managed service providers (MSPs) are companies that manage services for other companies by maintaining a range of processes and functions in order to improve operations and cut expenses. They could be involved in many facets of your business, from marketing to supply chain management to the deployment of utilities such as water and power.

Since this book is about cybersecurity, we'll focus on that aspect. MSPs make it possible for your company to outsource many of your security needs to an external organization. I've mentioned many cybersecurity functions that large companies have the resources to handle themselves, such as network monitoring, patch management, and cyber threat analysis, but if your business is a small- or medium-sized (SMS) business, it may be best to procure the services of an MSP.

Chief information security officers often work directly for the company whose networks they devote to securing. Those who don't often work for MSPs instead.

A typical MSP will offer a variety of different cybersecurity services, and when your company becomes a client, you can choose which of their services you need. Keeping your network secure requires constant, everyday work. Sometimes it may be appropriate to delegate some of that work to an MSP.

Here's a list of services most MSPs provide:

- Authentication management, assuring that user accounts and individual computers are authorized to access parts of your network by proving their identities.
- Bandwidth management, assuring that your network's capacity for data in transit is properly allocated for a variety of functions.
- Intrusion detection and intrusion prevention, to monitor your network activity for possible indicators of cyberattacks so they can be detected and prevented.
- Administering your on-premises and cloud servers to assure that they function securely; monitoring how they're used and configured, and assuring they have their latest security patches.
- Data backup and recovery, to assure your organization can retain sensitive and mission-critical data in the wake of ransomware and other sorts of cyberattacks.
- Technical support, being responsive to any technology problems your IT department and nontechnical employees encounter and doing their best to resolve them.
- Sometimes MSPs can augment your network with their own cloud servers and infrastructure, so some MSPs can offer both managed security services and also function as a cloud network provider.

Mitch Parker has some advice about MSPs from his experience as a CISO. I asked him when it is appropriate for an organization to hire a managed service provider. He thinks it's important "when the expenditure to address risks as part of a business does not either align with the current support organization within the information technology department or cannot be budgeted for." He further identifies situations when a company already outsources certain aspects of its IT department and if the company doesn't have around-the-clock support staff.

Parker also identified these signs of a good managed service provider:

- Excellent communication with the account management team
- Agreed-upon reports and metrics to provide insight into performance and improvements
- Ability to leverage existing security tools or use their own to support the organization
- Expertise with the business and information systems in use
- Ability to quickly respond to and address discovered issues
- Excellent service-level agreements to address any potential downtime issues

The Dark Web and Your Data

What happens on the dark web can have a direct impact on your business, regardless of its size or industry. As I write this book, I'm also doing cyber threat research for a major Canadian bank as a side gig. So, this is something I've been thinking about a lot lately.

What is the dark web, you might ask? There are two major proxy networks on the internet, Tor and I2P. Tor is especially popular. They both work pretty much the same way. You need special software on your PC or phone to access these networks. Data through these networks goes through multiple proxy servers between your computer and the internet server on the other end. Through each proxy server, your computer and the internet server are made anonymous. The dark web includes the parts of the web that can be accessed only through these networks, not through a conventional web browser, so it's difficult for law enforcement to track users on the dark web, although it can be done.

These technologies are perfectly legal in many areas of the world, although they are banned in China. They have legitimate uses; in fact, much of that technology was developed by people working for US government agencies. A legitimate use could involve a government spy who needs to share information with the agency they work for or a civilian journalist who needs to work in a hostile country. However, because of the anonymity features of Tor and I2P, they're also used to break the law. Legally speaking, in most countries, simply using Tor or I2P is legal. It's the many activities that occur over Tor or I2P, such as conducting illegal acts like selling substances or conducting cyberattacks.

Dark web markets are like eBay, but for illegal goods and services. In fact, they are more like eBay than you might guess. Anyone can be a buyer or seller. Customer and vendor accounts develop a reputation based on whether other buyers and sellers have found them to be trustworthy. No one wants to buy cocaine from a vendor who's known to sell baby powder.

If you're conducting legal business, you might think you wouldn't need to worry about the dark web. However, there are two major ways that dark web activity can harm your business and its data.

First, malware, phishing kits, exploits, and cybercrime services are sold on dark web markets. This has made it easier than ever for cyberattacks to harm your business because a cybercriminal doesn't need to know how to develop malware or exploits to use them. All they have to do is have enough cryptocurrency to buy the goods.

Second, a lot of the data that's exposed through data breaches ends up being sold on dark web markets and through dark web forums. One thing I've seen through my research is massive databases of credit card numbers, including card verification values (CVVs). Some vendors sell *Fullz*, which is identification data on individuals and companies that can be used for identity fraud or financial fraud. Your research and development data can be sold on the dark web, so can data about your bank accounts and authentication data for your online services.

In these two ways, dark web markets and forums are a threat to your business. Law enforcement investigation can be hit or miss and often results in a dark web market going offline while two more replace it. The best way to prevent the dark web from harming your business is to follow the cybersecurity advice in this book. Prevent cyber threats before they occur in the first place.

Security Leaders on Cyber Defense

I asked some business cybersecurity leaders for their advice on a few different defensive security topics. Remember that sometimes the best offense is a good defense. A security operations center (SOC), a cybersecurity team that's dedicated to actively monitoring your computer network for cyber threats, can help tremendously when it comes to preventing the harm of cyberattacks. It's something usually only large businesses can afford, but if your organization has the resources to support a SOC, here are some tips for you.

All of the cybersecurity leaders I asked agreed that security maturity and budget are big factors in determining whether your company is ready to support a SOC. According to Andrew Gish-Johnson, if you don't have the budget to staff a dedicated SOC with multiple full-time employees who cover business hours, you can get by with one employee "triaging events via email and phone." Due to the cost, Randy Marchany believes the organization "would have to be in a high-risk level and may consider themselves to be a high-value target that outsourcing to an MSSP [managed security service provider] is a risk itself." Additionally, according to Mitch Parker, the budget needs to include the infrastructure and the human resources and management personnel of a fully distributed SOC. The costs can keep small companies from being able to support a SOC.

When it comes to hiring for an SOC, Gish-Johnson believes successful help-desk employees are good candidates for advancing to cybersecurity positions in the SOC because their jobs at the help desk require "strong communication skills, the ability to learn the organization, and effective handling of the unexpected." Marchany emphasized diversity in skill level, perspective, and experience, and also believes that both internal and external candidates are important. Parker recommends a lot of up-front planning to determine exactly what kinds of employees a company needs: "Ideally, an organization will use the output from a risk analysis, gap analysis, and risk management plan to identify the skills needed, number of analysts and managers required, and development plans for them to continue to learn and grow."

I also asked these same cybersecurity professionals about whether an organization should invest in a SIEM, and they did not all agree. Bassi and Marchany agreed that yes, they should, to keep teams from burning out due to the volume of data and to make sure all data is stored properly in case it needs to be accessed at a later time. Jeremy Dean, Gish-Johnson, and Parker were less supportive. Dean's concern is the expense involved for small companies, but he believes that its benefit may offset the expense. Gish-Johnson thinks parts of a SIEM can be implemented, such as log aggregation or an IT ticketing system, especially in a lean organization. Parker believes that it's valuable if a company can support it, but there are possibilities for outsourcing:

> "With the current explosion of data set to continue exponentially, it is not economically feasible for organizations to continue to invest in their own SIEM unless they have the resources to scale to these higher levels. With that, we recommend that even higher-level businesses invest in MSSP and cloud-based relationships to be able to ingest and process the amounts of data needed to identify potential threats to the environment."

If your organization is too small to support a SOC and a SIEM, there are other, more affordable ways to watch your network for cyber threats. In smaller companies, your network administrator can look for indications of compromise with log analysis software and other network monitoring tools.

Control Your Data

Controlling your data is an essential step for improving your organization's cybersecurity. Understand the ways data can be threatened as they impact confidentiality, integrity, and availability. Implement effective access control systems based on the principle of least privilege. Make sure that every act to your data is properly logged and traceable to a specific human being. Guard the physical security of your precious data assets by understanding how to prevent unauthorized parties from being able to touch your computers and any other means of exchanging data, both digital and on printed paper. Understand malware and prevent infections in order to protect your data from spyware, ransomware, and related threats. Implement the best cryptography you possibly can. You should also make sure as much of your data as possible is encrypted. If bring your own device or working from home is necessary, security harden your organization accordingly with the right policies and security controls. Make sure your security team understands the threat dark web activity can pose to your data through the selling of breached data and the sale of malware, exploits, and cyberattack services. Ensuring the best cybersecurity throughout your organization is the best way you can mitigate this threat.

The right security team can be vigilant. They can understand the various important factors when it comes to protecting your data, and they can engage in the everyday work that's required to maintain security.

Chapter 7
Step 7: Understand the Human Factor

One common misconception about cybersecurity is that it's all technical. Yes, computer software and hardware are always important factors in preventing and mitigating cyberattacks. Software vulnerabilities succumb to exploitation. Poorly designed hardware is easier to hack. But newcomers to our field tend to overlook the human factor.

Cybercrime groups target human beings and our foolishness. It's much more difficult to acquire malicious access to an internal computer in a network by confusing firewalls and cracking encryption. It's much easier to trick a human being who has the username and password to an account with privileged access.

The majority of cyberattacks my colleagues and I see involve social engineering at some point or another. Social engineering is the art of fooling people, and understanding it is one of the most important areas of cybersecurity.

User interfaces (UIs) are the computer graphics that help you to interact with your favorite software applications. They're the buttons you click and the menus you tap. They run in your operating system, and they exist all throughout the web as well. Interestingly, when user interfaces have poor visual design or confusing wording, those mistakes can cause cybersecurity problems. If your company develops software, I'll explain how crucial it is that you create user interfaces that help users make good security decisions. If your company doesn't develop software, you can at least train your employees to understand how to use bad UI more effectively. I'll explain why good UI and user experience (UX) design is important, how it's relevant to cybersecurity, and what you can do to reduce cybersecurity risk. I'll also explain why it helps to understand psychology and sociology as you work to improve your organization's cybersecurity.

Many cyber exploits are internal in nature. That means they're conducted by people who work for your company. They're conducted by people who were given usernames, passwords, physical keys, and access to your building *legitimately,* because they're supposed to have it in order to work for your company. I have some advice about how to prevent internal cyberattacks. Some of my advice is the common wisdom of my industry, and the rest of my advice you'll likely never read anywhere else. I have some unconventional thinking about this problem.

Finally, we'll consider hacktivism and its potential impact to your business. Most cyberattacks are financially motivated. Hacktivism is the one notable exception. Hacktivists aren't motivated by money; they're motivated by social activism. If you've ever heard of Anonymous, seen their Guy Fawkes masks, and heard the motto "We are Anonymous, we do not forgive, we do not forget," then you know of at least one hacktivism group. There are many others. And hacktivism is also conducted by individuals who don't belong to a group.

Always consider the human factor in your company's cybersecurity. That's what this step is all about.

Social Engineering

Social engineering is all about fooling people. Today's social engineering attacks often use websites, emails, and malware. It's easy to think social engineering attacks require some sort of mastery of computer science. But really, social engineering is much of the same sort of trickery that has existed throughout human civilization long before computers were ever invented.

Consider Trojans, one of the most common types of malware. Trojan malware works by fooling a human being into thinking that a malicious file or application is something they want. It's possible to file-bind malware to a cute picture of kittens and attach it to an email. The malware will execute when the human target tries to open the image. They think it's something they want. Who doesn't love kittens, right? In the 1990s and early 2000s, people were often tempted to download packs of fun screensavers and novelty cursors for their Windows PCs. But that adorable freeware wasn't actually "free." The cost of admission was granting a cybercriminal malicious access to a computer.

Sometimes Trojans appeal to utility rather than fun or cuteness. Office workers are sometimes targeted by people who email them by entities who pretend to be co-workers or company stakeholders with important office documents, such as text documents, spreadsheets, or PDF files. Just like photos of kittens, those documents can also have malware attached to them.

One of the more common ways that Trojan malware is distributed these days is as fun or useful mobile apps, targeting iPhones or Android phones. Apple and Google work hard to prevent Trojans from appearing in their app stores, but sometimes they haven't been successful.

So, why do we call them Trojans? The origin of the name is in Ancient Greek myth. During the Trojan War, the city of Troy was attacked by the Achaeans. Trojan means "of Troy." Much of this tale was told through Homer's *The Iliad*. Toward the end of the Trojan War, the Achaeans found a clever way to penetrate Troy's mighty fortified city. Trying to break Troy's walls with spears and swords would be exhausting and fruitless. The most effective way in was through deceiving the Trojan guards. The Achaeans did this with their Trojan horse: a massive wooden trophy with their soldiers hidden inside. Once they were let into the Trojan fortress, the soldiers were ready to attack, so it didn't matter how well built the fortress was. Additionally, the guards were not a hindrance because they could be fooled.

Homer died in the year 651 BC. Trojan malware wouldn't be invented until nearly 2,000 years later, but the psychological tactics are the same. Although technology has evolved over the centuries, human nature has not.

In step 1, I described how Kevin Mitnick, one of the world's most notorious cyberattackers, conducted his notable cyberattacks by deceiving people. He tricked a bus driver into giving him a ticket punch. He phoned receptionists while pretending to be a co-worker or tech support. Those are also classic social engineering tactics. In fact, when social engineering attacks are conducted through telephone, we call that *phreaking*.

My friend Jenny Radcliffe is one of the top social engineering experts in the cybersecurity industry. She runs a firm called Human Factor Security, which investigates social engineering attacks and conducts training programs. You can learn more about Jenny and her work at `https://humanfactorsecurity.co.uk`. I interviewed her to learn from her expertise in this area. You can read the interview in "A Chat with Human Factor Security Expert Jenny Radcliffe."

A Chat with Human Factor Security Expert Jenny Radcliffe

Kim Crawley: What are some misconceptions organizations have about social engineering attacks?

Jenny Radcliffe: I think the biggest misconception is that if they educate people about phishing, then they have tried their best. Many organizations still think that social engineering basically *is* phishing when it, of course, has many applications and much wider reach than just email-based approaches.

Crawley: Are cybersecurity professionals targeted by social engineering differently than laypeople are? Do we overestimate our ability to succumb?

Radcliffe: It depends on the social engineer, the target, and the approach. A good social engineer will tailor their methods to the target and make the attack bespoke to have a better chance of success. It all depends on the amount of effort and skill someone wants to apply to a job. Like anything else, there are talented people on either end of the moral spectrum, and there are others who are lazier and occasionally get lucky. Cybersecurity professionals *do* need targeting differently in as much as anyone needs profiling based on their job, personality, and history to be targeted effectively.

The profession is vulnerable in thinking we can't be hit as easily as I see social engineering within the sector all the time. For example, there is a lot of catphishing going on to make connections in the industry, and people are mined for their connections and resources by aspiring "influencers" within the industry. They don't tend to notice because flattery is powerful, but if you look closely, it's obvious to see. I'd say the industry is regularly socially engineered by snake oil and fake experts, for whom the only actual social engineering that is going on is convincing people they are something they are not.

Crawley: I have a feeling that most cyberattacks involve social engineering. Is that true?

Radcliffe: Yes, and the statistics tend to bear this out. So, depending on where you look, anything from up to 95 percent of cyberattacks involves some form of social engineering. Of course, it depends on how you define this but inasmuch as social engineering involves deceiving, manipulating, or exploiting humans, then it is pretty much behind every attack in one way or another.

Crawley: Have social engineering tactics evolved over the years?

(Continues)

(Continued)

Radcliffe: Malicious social engineering exploits human weaknesses and exploits human psychological tendencies and traits to the detriment of the target—that fact will always be the same and remain unchanged, regardless of what point in technical or human history we happen to be at. The method of delivery might change and adapt to the wider cultural narrative, such as Covid-19, or with advances in technology, as with deep fakes, but the goals and ultimate levers remain the same.

[Deep fakes are videos that look completely authentic but are actually fake. They use artificial intelligence machine learning technology to make well-known people look like they're saying or doing things they've actually never done in real life. Some of the earliest examples of deep fake videos simulated Facebook's Mark Zuckerberg saying incriminating things. The deep fake phenomenon means that not even realistic-looking videos can be trusted.]

Crawley: What can organizations do to prevent social engineering exploits?

Radcliffe: They need to educate people first that cons, scams, and fraud are now facilitated through technology and that they need to be alert and aware that they may be targeted both individually and as part of the wider organization. People need to be educated and shown how to comply with basic cyber hygiene (such as application updates and password usage) and encouraged to discuss the topic freely as part of the wider organizational objectives rather than as an add-on. In terms of my attacker perspective, the best thing we could encourage people to do to be more secure is to stop posting every detail of their life on social media. As a tool for spear phishing, it's the single biggest thing I can exploit.

Crawley: Has the dark web made it easier for cybercriminals to engage in social engineering?

Radcliffe: In some ways yes, as it's easy to buy the technical tools and basic information we need to carry out attacks and generally snoop on people these days, but the skill and finesse required to persist with a targeted social engineering attack are both difficult to learn and to define, so buying it off a shelf, even in a marketplace specializing in crime, is still not that easy.

Crawley: Is it useful to think of cyber social engineering like old-fashioned scams?

Radcliffe: I'd say so. I consider myself first and foremost an old-fashioned con artist who constructs my scams using the tools available to me. I think it helps people to think of cybercrime with a human element, as it's not so nebulous as a virus or malware somewhere online. It also makes it less scary, as a human, however malicious, can be stopped, tracked, and potentially held responsible. It's an accurate description and takes some of the potency away from an often-misunderstood concept, so yes, I find it useful to describe social engineering in this way.

Phishing

It's time to get into phishing, a topic I've mentioned a few times already. Phishing involves the use of emails, text messages, social media posts, or websites to imitate trusted entities to acquire sensitive data or access from their targets.

Here's an example: A person has a checking account with Acme Bank. They often use Acme Bank's online banking website and mobile app to pay bills and check their bank account balance. They use their username and password to log into their bank account. Protecting this information is crucial, because if a cybercriminal acquires it, they can steal money from their account.

The person receives an email that appears to be from Acme Bank. The sender's address is `support@àcmebank.com`. The body of the email uses the unique graphical style of an email from Acme Bank, corporate logo, and everything. It says:

> In order to protect your account with Acme Bank online banking, you will need to change your password. Click this link and log in as soon as possible. This needs to be done quickly because "hackers" may be able to acquire access to your account.

The link takes a person to a web page that looks just like an authentic Acme Bank web page, with `www.àcmebank.com` in the address bar of their web browser. They input their username and password into a web form, along with a new password.

They think they've secured their account. But in fact, they have unwittingly given cybercriminals access to their account because the email was a phishing email and the web page was a phishing web page. The website belonged to the cyberattackers, and now they have their victim's username and password.

URLs and their domain names have to be unique. If I were a cybercriminal, I couldn't make a website with `www.google.com` or a fake Gmail account with `www.gmail.com`, because Google owns those domain names. They were registered years ago. But what a cybercriminal can do is try to register `www.ġoogle.com` and `www.ġmail.com`. If you look carefully, you may be able to see that those domains don't have the usual "g" or "m" (but you also may not be able to tell). I used Unicode characters, which provide support for a multitude of non-English languages in computer applications. The `g` and `ġ` are different but similar-looking characters. My fictitious cybercriminal couldn't use `www.acmebank.com` because it was already taken by the legitimate (fictional) Acme Bank. So, the cybercriminal registered `www.àcmebank.com` instead. We call this a *punicode* attack. It's a way cyberattackers can trick their victims into thinking that the domain names in their phishing emails and web pages are authentic.

Cybercriminals don't even have to be good at web design or graphic design to craft phishing emails and web pages these days.

Dark web markets sell phishing kits. They contain all the web and graphic design work that's needed to properly imitate a trusted entity—a particular bank, utility company, employer, government agency, media streaming service, video game service—any sort of business where a victim may be a customer and whom a customer trusts with their sensitive data.

Phishing kits and punicode attacks make phishing easy as pie. *And I know cybersecurity experts can be fooled too.* So, I never click links in emails from my bank or utility companies or social networks or media streaming services or Amazon. I launch my web browser and type their URL directly into my address bar. All legitimate companies online will allow you to manage your accounts with them that way. You never have to click a link in an email to do anything you must do with the service. I've also received phishing text messages from my bank. I've done the right thing and never clicked them. Even if I don't input my username and password into a web form, a malicious link in a phishing text or email can download malware onto my PC or phone. Don't do it!

What Can NFTs and ABA Teach Us About Social Engineering?

I'm writing this in 2021, and nonfungible tokens (NFTs) are all the rage online. So, what is an NFT? An NFT is a new phenomenon where sellers promise to sell you access to a digital file (usually an image file, but not always) in exchange for lots of money. I've seen NFTs sell for thousands to millions of dollars. If they're so expensive, they must be super valuable, right? No, not really. Not at all, actually. NFTs are a scam.

NFTs are records on blockchains, the kind of blockchains that record transactions on popular cryptocurrencies such as Bitcoin or Ethereum. In fact, NFTs often use the same blockchains that are used by cryptocurrencies. They point to the address of a file on the internet. But anyone with the URL to the file can access it; they needn't spend millions of dollars on an NFT. I could sell an NFT to the Wikipedia page on NFTs at `https://en.wikipedia.org/wiki/Non-fungible_token`. But the buyer of my NFT would have no actual ownership of the web page. And Wikipedia's administrators could delete the web page at any time because it belongs to them, not the NFT buyer. Rich people's willingness to spend thousands or millions of dollars on NFTs doesn't represent the NFT's value; it reveals their gullibility.

I remember as a teenager in 1999, seeing a mall vendor sell deeds to moon property. I was tempted to buy one until someone advised me not to. Yes, the moon is real, just like the digital file an NFT is linked to. But no country or organization on Earth has any legal framework for claiming moon property. I can't sue someone for stealing my plot of land on the moon as I can with a plot of land on Earth. Those moon deeds are essentially a scam, just like NFTs.

Unlike with NFTs, being tricked into buying a moon deed doesn't do much environmental harm, but NFTs cause loads of environmental harm. The amount of electricity needed to generate one NFT is immense because multiple potential sellers compete for each NFT. Since only a minority of power generation in the world is from relatively clean means like wind, solar, and nuclear, much of the power used to generate an NFT causes pollution. As Justine Calma wrote for *The Verge*:

> Akten, a digital artist, had analyzed 18,000 NFTs and found that the average NFT has a carbon footprint somewhat lower than Space Cat's but still equivalent to more than a month's worth of electricity for a person living in the EU.

Most of that electricity is generated in ways that pollute skies and accelerate climate change, as does the booming phenomenon of the cryptocurrency generation itself. Humanity is making NFTs and mining cryptocurrency in ways that are destroying our planet.

A few clever people on Twitter have posted tweets with an image of someone right-clicking an image and clicking Save As with the caption "How to terrify an NFT-loving tech bro." There is truth to this meme. NFTs don't grant you access to a file online; anyone can access it for free. You can download graphics on the web for free, and the actual owner of the file can remove it from the web anytime, but they can't delete the image download from your hard drive.

Money doesn't buy common sense. The NFT phenomenon shows how people can be socially engineered into spending millions of dollars on nothing. The social engineers are the celebrities and artists who are hyping this scam to make money for themselves. Frankly, I believe someone who clicks a link in a phishing email is much less of a sucker.

Now let's talk about ABA. ABA stands for applied behavioral analysis. The whole philosophy behind ABA is that autistic people aren't *people* with thoughts and feelings of our own. It's the evil belief that we're subhuman and need to be punished or "rewarded" into behaving the way an abusive ABA practitioner wants us to behave. ABA inventor Ole Ivar Lovaas said:

> You see, you start pretty much from scratch when you work with an autistic child. You have a person in the physical sense—they have hair, a nose and a mouth—but they are not people in the psychological sense. One way to look at the job of helping autistic kids is to see it as a matter of constructing a person. You have the raw materials, but you have to build the person.

And how did he try to "build the person"? Here's what he said:

> We stay close to them and when they hurt themselves, we scream "no" as loud as we can, and we look furious and at the same time we shock them. What typically happens is this—we shock the child once and he stops for about 30 seconds and then he tries it again.

And he meant *shock*. He was saying he electrocutes the child. The Judge Rotenburg Center in Massachusetts has been known to electrocute autistic children for decades. Such electrocution is not only deeply emotionally traumatic, but it can injure and even kill. It's absolutely horrific.

Even though Association for Behavior Analysis International, the organization that "regulates" ABA, endorses the Rotenburg Center in its conferences, ABA practitioners will often try to deny electrocution. They believe, "That's the old ABA. We've evolved since then!"

But mainstream psychology has long since abandoned behaviorism, the school of thought ABA is based on. People aren't their behaviors. Behaviors are caused by thoughts, feelings, and medical conditions. A teenager who spends an entire day sleeping isn't necessarily being "naughty." They may have mononucleosis, a virus that causes extreme fatigue. A child isn't refusing to eat a sandwich because they're "bad"; maybe they're allergic to peanuts. A dyslexic child doesn't avoid their assignment in English class because they're "lazy"; they have a neurological condition that makes it difficult to read.

Even when ABA practitioners don't electrocute or hit, it's still abuse. Denying a child access to their favorite teddy bear until they do something that's painful to them is deeply abusive. Children will also be "rewarded" with candies and treats. That all teaches them that their thoughts and feelings don't matter and that their bodies don't belong to them. They cannot act unless an adult tells them to through punishments and "rewards." Good dog trainers say they wouldn't even treat a dog like that; it's abusive.[1]

Children who are put through ABA have been found to have PTSD and may become victims of sexual exploitation. Sexual exploitation can teach children that their bodies don't belong to them and that they should never say no to an adult.

I didn't write this book for a cookie or to avoid being spanked. I wrote this book because I'm intrinsically motivated to do so. Intrinsic motivation is behavior that's driven by internal rewards. I do it because it's naturally satisfying. This book was my idea, made of information I enjoy sharing with you. My cybersecurity writing career is driven by my self-actualization. The paycheck is just a necessary bonus that I require under capitalism.

---

[1] https://neuroclastic.com/2019/03/27/is-aba-really-dog-training-for-children-a-professional-dog-trainer-weighs-in/

I have never learned anything through behaviorist methods. I learn because I'm interested in the information. So do you. Anyone who has ever crammed for an exam they didn't care about, only to forget the content the moment the exam has been written, can understand why.

Lovaas, through the Feminine Boy Project, is also the inventor of gay conversion "therapy." Autism is just as natural as homosexuality and being transgender. You cannot "train" any of it out of a person; doing so is abusive.

So, what does this have to do with social engineering?

Well, through social engineering, the ABA industry has made its methods the primary autism "treatment," often funded by insurance companies and government agencies. The moment a child is diagnosed as autistic, they're told by presumed experts that their child will never use the toilet or talk or hold down a job unless they put them through this "lifesaving therapy." They must use early intervention and do it as soon as possible, before it's too late. These presumed experts often have medical degrees. It's a psychological "appeal to authority" tactic. And it also appeals to parental fear, the fear of disability, the bigotry of ableism. The ABA industry has socially engineered a problem that doesn't actually exist for which they have the "best" solution.

Through many years of activism, the gay community and the transgender community have fought the Lovaas-invented conversion "therapies" that abuse their own. Some countries, states, and provinces are making the practice illegal, and rightfully so. I truly wish that autistic conversion "therapy" were next.

As you see, the dangers of social engineering extend far beyond cyberattacks. They permeate many facets of society. People are being fooled into abusing their children and destroying our planet through NFTs to buy things they don't even actually own. Through "experts" and celebrities, fear and greed. It's much the same way cyberattackers appeal to authority by pretending to be your bank or utility company, appeal to fear by saying, "You must click here or bad stuff will happen," or appeal to greed by saying, "You won a prize! Click here!"

When you start seeing the world as social engineering researchers do, you can better understand how cyberattackers see success through human manipulation.

How to Prevent Social Engineering Attacks on Your Business

Everyone is susceptible to social engineering. All of your workers, from your nontechnical staff to your highly technical cybersecurity professionals, including you and your executives, can succumb to it. Even I can be fooled. Therefore, everyone needs social engineering training to avoid these attacks.

Give everyone in your organization social engineering training once or twice per year. Show your people what phishing emails, text messages, and websites can look like. Explain punicode attacks. Let people know that phishing can look exactly like legitimate emails, text messages, and websites.

Encourage your employees to always go to the websites of their service providers by entering URLs in their web browser, not by clicking links in messages that are potentially malicious.

Then there's phreaking, social engineering through the phone. Train your staff to never give sensitive information over the phone under any circumstances.

Cyberattackers will often pretend to be people who work in your organization. So you must have policies and assure everyone they will never be penalized in any way for being distrustful of people on the phone or in emails and text messages, no matter who they say they are, even if they say they're the IT department or the CEO. If sharing sensitive information or granting privileged access is absolutely necessary, it can be requested through a personal meeting or a video conference that proves the person is who they say they are. Well, the latter will work until deep fake technology gets more advanced.

Remind the people who may think they are too smart for social engineering, your technical staff, that they are especially attractive targets due to their network access and authority. Even people with CISSPs and PhDs in computer science can be fooled. Understanding that you can be deceived is the first step in preventing deception. This is an interesting paradox that I've found to be true.

In the office, email attachments must often be opened. Remind your staff to only open attachments from senders they recognize. Some email malware may still slip through the cracks. So, run updated antivirus software on their endpoint computers and implement malware detection in your email servers as much as you possibly can.

UI and UX Design

If you're reading this in an ebook format, your application has buttons for skipping chapters, brightening and dimming the screen, and changing the font size; an indicator of which page you're on; and the ability to swipe the pages with your finger, as if it was a printed book.

Your other applications also have buttons to click or menus to tap. These are all the basic elements of UI design. If it's done well, you can understand how to interact with it without any explanation. Effective UI design is full of visual clues. It should be intuitive.

UX incorporates UI design and goes beyond that. Is the application fast or slow? How do you feel while using the application? Can you do what you need to do with the application quickly and easily? Good UX design makes applications as enjoyable and pleasant to use as possible.

Here's where cybersecurity comes in. People can act in ways that are bad for security if UI and UX are done the wrong way.

Confusing UI can cause you to delete files when you don't intend to, threatening the integrity and availability components of the CIA triad. Security-minded UI design will show a series of asterisks on your screen instead of the characters you're entering when you input a password, just in case someone is watching.

UX comes into play in encouraging users to act in a secure way. The most effective authentication involves multiple factors—a password, a two-factor authentication (2FA) code application, and possibly an iris or fingerprint scan as well. Users will be less likely to use multiple factors of authentication when you make them difficult to use and make them have to input these methods more often than is convenient. Or they may be encouraged to log into an account with administrative privileges if they can't do their work in the application with limited privileges. You shouldn't need admin rights to switch your app's UI from light mode to dark mode, for instance.

Back in 2017, I wrote about a cyber threat caused by bad UI and UX design for AT&T Cybersecurity's blog.

> ASUSWRT's GUI contained two settings in the firewall section that were written as "Enable Web Access from WAN: No" and "Enable Firewall: Yes." Unfortunately, even if "Enable Firewall" was set to "No," public internet access to the router's admin panel would still be granted, even if "Enable Web Access from WAN" was set to "No." Even I, with my network administration experience, would find that confusing.

In a nutshell, the router settings were very confusing. Even a network security professional could be stumped. Designing the UI to clearly explain the settings to a user would empower them to configure their router more securely.

If your company develops software, you should learn about effective UI and UX design, which encourages users to engage in better cybersecurity behavior. If your company doesn't develop software, your security team should look through the applications you use and make sure your employees understand how to use them properly.

Internal Threats

Organizations are often focused on external threats. Those are cyber threats that originate from outside of your company from people who don't work for your organization. They're outside of your supply chain. They're cybercriminals from the outside who chose your company as a target. It's the most classic example of a cyberattack: a big, bad cyberattacker in a hoodie finds your company's website with dollar signs in their eyes and tries to break in.

Those sorts of incidents definitely do happen, although the hoodie-wearing "hacker" is a stereotype more than anything else. Cyberattackers can look like anyone; they can be wearing anything. They may even be wearing a military uniform, because a lot of cyberattacks come from nation-state military groups. You definitely need to secure your network's perimeter and make sure malicious actors from the outside can't break it.

But internal cyberattackers are often overlooked. These cyberattacks come from people who work for your company. It's easier for internal cyberattackers to exploit your network because they don't have to break through your perimeter. You've already invited them inside because they need that access to perform their jobs. They often don't need to escalate their privileges because their user accounts may already have the privileges they need in order to do damage.

Internal cyberattacks are alarmingly common. Because of the privileged access that insiders already have, they can be a lot more difficult to detect and stop than outsider threats. When an employee is working with sensitive data, it's difficult to know whether they are doing something malicious. If an insider behaves maliciously within your network, they can claim it was an honest mistake, and it can be challenging to prove guilt.

Insider threats can also be a lot more difficult to contain than outsider threats. According to Ponemon Institute's 2018 Cost of Insider Threats study, it took an average of 73 days to contain insider incidents. Only 16 percent of insider incidents were contained in less than 30 days. Even if a threat to your network lasted 20 days, imagine how much harm could be done in that time.

I'm covering this topic in this step, because mitigating internal cyber threats is largely a social concept. And when it comes to preventing internal attacks, I will share some common industry wisdom and my unconventional ideas.

First, you need to watch for disgruntled employees. The most dangerous are those who have received termination notices. They may decide that they have nothing to lose because they aren't worried about getting fired anymore. Depending on the nature of your organization and the work you do, it might be a good idea for them to stop working for your company the moment they know they've been terminated. Get them to give you any physical keys they might have and disable their user accounts right away. It may ultimately cost your organization less money to just give your terminated employee their severance pay than to pay them to work a few extra weeks. But if they must work for some time after they've been terminated, watch them especially carefully.

Disgruntled employees who aren't set to be terminated may also pose a threat. Signs of disgruntled employees who may become malicious insiders include those who have frequent conflicts with supervisors and co-workers and those who demonstrate declined performance and general tardiness. Visits to websites with job listings are another clear indication of a disgruntled employee.

Interestingly, another type of employee or contractor who could be a malicious insider is one who seems unusually enthusiastic about their work. They may volunteer for more work or additional tasks not because they want a raise but because they want to expand their access to sensitive data. They may say, "Yes, I work the help desk, but I have lots of experience with managing networks. I can fill in for the network administrator when they're taking time off."

Frequent trips to other cities or countries can be a sign of industrial espionage. They could be sharing sensitive and proprietary information with another company.

Another major indicator of insider threat actors involves employees or staff who have had significant unexplained changes to their financial circumstances. Why is that employee who makes $40,000 per year driving a Bentley all of a sudden? Or the indicators may be a lot more subtle than that. Either way, the extra money could be coming from industrial espionage, cryptomining malware, or stealing money from corporate accounts.

Second, you need to monitor your employee's user accounts. Log analysis software, application firewalls, and security information and event management systems (SIEM) can be used to watch for user account behavior anomalies. Examples of anomalies are user accounts being active at times your employee doesn't usually work, or if their user account accesses files, folders, applications, or servers they don't usually access. User account behavior anomalies aren't always indications of cyberattack. Maybe your employee just needs to perform a task they don't often do. A strong security team watching for network security events can leverage network device logs and possibly a SIEM to determine which events are false positives and which events are true positive indications of compromise (IOC).

Now here's my unconventional wisdom—advice you're unlikely to hear elsewhere and may be politically controversial. One of the best ways you can prevent internal cyberattacks is to treat your employees and contractors well and pay them well. In my opinion, a happy employee is a loyal employee and one who is less likely to want to harm their employer. Plus, if they're well paid, they're less likely to be motivated to engage in "extracurricular activities" to make extra money on the side through actions like cryptomining and selling sensitive company data.

Also, don't interfere with worker unionization, and be willing to negotiate with a union if your employees join one. Some companies spend millions of dollars trying to monitor and intimidate their employees to dissuade them from unionization. These actions can be considered morally wrong and a waste of resources that could be better allocated to improving your organization's cybersecurity and productivity. Further, you will be damaging employee morale. Don't be an example of "beatings will continue until morale improves." Treating your employees well makes them happy, and happy employees are naturally more productive and produce better-quality work. A company that treats their workers well has nothing to fear from unionization because they will already be giving them what a union typically wants in the negotiation process.

Regardless, no organization deserves internal cyberattacks. An unlocked vehicle in a parking lot doesn't deserve to be robbed, but on the other hand, locking your doors isn't guaranteed auto theft prevention. But it's still a good idea to lock your car doors. And occasionally, even a company that treats their employees well can face internal cyberattacks because human nature can be unpredictable. But you can definitely reduce the likelihood of internal cyberattacks by treating your workers well.

Addressing internal cyber threats requires both types of work—watching your employees for indications of internal threats (but not to prevent unionization) and treating them well to improve morale.

Hacktivism

Hacktivists are cyberattackers that are politically motivated rather than financially motivated. The majority of cyberattacks are financially motivated, whether they're external or internal. Those that aren't financially motivated are almost always hacktivism. Hacktivism is a minor threat, but it's one all organizations must be aware of.

Here's an example of hacktivism. An ecommerce website sells fur coats. An animal rights group doesn't like that very much because the fur trade encourages an industry that kills animals for the sake of fashion. The animal rights group knocks the ecommerce website offline for a while with a distributed denial-of-service (DDoS) attack. Then they vandalize the website by putting images of slaughtered animals and the words "fur is murder" on every web page. They don't make any money from doing this, but they've harmed the fur business and used their site to make a political point.

Hacktivism is sometimes done by individuals, but it's more often done by organized groups. They can be people with altruistic goals: animal rights groups, environmentalists, people who dislike capitalism. Or they could be groups with more negative goals: people from the far right who are motivated by racism, sexism, homophobia, transphobia, ableism, or antisemitism.

Depending on the kind of work your business does, it could be considered offensive by different ideological groups. A strong defensive security team should be able to identify which groups of people could be motivated to do harm to your organization for different political reasons.

Sometimes a hacktivism group will have differing motives and campaigns over time. Anonymous is perhaps the most famous hacktivism group, although there are many others. There is no formal, verifiable membership in hacktivist groups like Anonymous or LulzSec. They aren't like biker gangs with a formal membership process and violent retribution toward those who wear their "colors" without permission from group leadership. Anyone who performs an act and says they're Anonymous or LulzSec *is* Anonymous or LulzSec, or from a similar hacktivist group. This tendency can especially be traced to Anonymous. The origin of the name came from the 4chan web forums in the early 2000s. In 4chan culture, users are encouraged to post without providing a username, so everyone is named "anonymous." The culture of 4chan thrives when posts can't be traced to a particular user. Not being linked to "real names" isn't enough; you mustn't know that the author of one post also authored another. Anonymous's activity started on 4chan.

This step covers many human psychological and sociological topics that must be considered in your organization's cybersecurity. Remember that cybersecurity is ultimately more psychological and sociological than technological, although the technological aspect is also important. Computers are used and abused by human beings, and understanding them and their motivations may help you improve your cybersecurity and protect your valuable assets.

Chapter 8
Step 8: Build Redundancy and Resilience

One of the most important things your business can do to thrive in the ever-evolving cyber threat landscape is to assure that your data and computer systems have the capacity, bandwidth, and redundancy to weather any storm you may encounter. A storm can be figurative and occur in the form of a brutal series of cyberattacks, but a storm can also be literal. What if a natural disaster hits your datacenter, factory, or corporate office? In this final step, you'll be thinking like a Girl Scout (or Girl Guide, in my country): always be prepared!

The data your business stores is essential for its survival. That includes the software applications your company uses, financial records, network logs, authentication credentials, reports, research and development, employee records, stakeholder documentation, inventory systems—the list goes on and on. Cyberattacks are inevitable, and they can threaten the integrity and availability of your mission-critical applications and records. There are also accidental risks, such as human error, natural disasters, and electrical power problems. You must prepare for anything that can happen.

Understanding Data and Networks

For the purposes of this chapter, I must define some terminology you may not have seen before. Endpoints are the PCs, mobile devices, and internet of things (IoT) devices that people use to interact with computer networks. The PC in someone's cubicle and the iPhone in your pocket are both endpoints. Servers are the machines that operate services through computer networks. Servers can be on your company's own premises, or they can be far away from your premises and hosted by a cloud provider. More and more organizations these days are using cloud providers. These are platforms such as Amazon Web Services, Microsoft Azure, and Linode. There are hundreds of cloud providers out there, although the ones I've mentioned are some of the most popular.

Your local network provides the way for the endpoints in your workplace to communicate with each other. It exists entirely inside your office or home regardless of whether it's wired or wireless. The main vector of any local network is your router. Think of your router as an airport and your endpoints and local peripherals as aircraft. Your local network is known as a *local area network* (LAN), and if your LAN uses WiFi, it's a wireless *local area network* (WLAN). Most LANs and WLANs connect with the world's largest network, the internet, but they don't have to connect to the internet to be a LAN. If an endpoint in your LAN communicates with the internet, it does so through your router. Many LANs also contain printers, scanners, fax machines, photocopiers, and network-attached storage (NAS). If your PC endpoint sends a document to your local printer, it sends data to your printer through your router (if it's networked), but it doesn't go through the internet. The network transmission is contained in your LAN.

If you're working from home, your LAN could also be called a *personal area network* (PAN). This is relatively new terminology. A PAN is used and administrated by a single person, but you may also share it with a spouse or your children. It consists of your router and the endpoints you're likely to have at home—a PC, a MacBook, video game consoles, phones, tablets, home entertainment systems, smart TVs, smart speakers, and so on.

Now let's leave home and get back to your company's professional workplace, whether it's an office, factory, retail store, restaurant, academic campus, hospital, or industrial plant. If there are server machines in your building, whether they go through your LAN, through the internet, or both, then you have an *on-premises* network.

There are also other types of networks your office and on-premises network can have. A *campus area network* (CAN) connects multiple buildings, but its coverage area is smaller than a city or town. Like the name implies, CANs are typically found on college or university campuses, but they can also be used for private businesses that have multiple buildings in an area that resembles a college campus. They're also sometimes found in K–12 schools and hospital campuses.

That leads to the next type of network, a *metropolitan area network* (MAN). These are the networks that span the approximate area of a city, but to fit the definition, they must be administrated by a single company or organization. Sometimes a city government can be that organization, but private businesses can have MANs too.

A *wide area network* (WAN) covers an area larger than a city. If your organization has its own network that spans Toronto, London, and Los Angeles, for example, you have a WAN. The largest WAN is the internet, and you probably use it every day.

If you have storage devices that connect with your on-premises servers without going through a LAN, MAN, or WAN, you may call it a *storage area network* (SAN).

Virtual private networks (VPN) are defined by how they implement cryptography, rather than by the number of machines that connect to them or the size of the area they serve. A VPN can be any size, from a VPN in your own home that serves six endpoints to a VPN you run through every continent on Earth. If you like watching YouTube or listening to podcasts, you've probably heard commercials for consumer VPN providers, such as NordVPN or ExpressVPN. Your business can also run its own VPN and have it be used by your organization exclusively. A VPN encrypts your communications through any type of network, including the internet, to protect your data from cyberattackers and other possibly hostile entities while it is in transit. As I've mentioned, if your business has people working from home who connect to your company's own network, you should definitely deploy your own VPN for them. If you don't know how to do that, your knowledgeable IT department or security team can help you.

So, you have endpoints, on-premises networks, and different classifications of networks that could be on premises or elsewhere. You know what a cloud provider is. What if you combine your organization's on-premises network with a cloud network? You get a *hybrid* cloud network. It's a popular option for many types of businesses these days.

Now that we understand many of the different ways your computers and networks can be implemented, we will explore ways your organization can build redundancy and resilience.

Building Capacity and Scalability with the Power of the Cloud

When Disney+ was launched in November 2019, I used the new streaming media service on day one. It was great to be able to watch *DuckTales* and *Darkwing Duck* on any of my endpoints whenever I wanted. During the first day, I was one of millions of other consumers who noticed that our video streams were slow or interrupted. It was frustrating.

Within days, Disney apologized for its new service's unreliable performance, and it fixed the problem literally overnight. All of a sudden, I found Disney+ ran smoothly and quickly, without any buffering or other such frustrations. Other consumers also noticed that the service greatly improved its network performance. There was probably a comparable number of consumers using the service later that week as there was on day one. The demand likely didn't decrease; the data supply increased.

How did Disney fix the problem so quickly? I have zero insider information about how Disney and its various companies operate, but

I can speculate on what happened. Disney went to its cloud provider and immediately expanded its network capacity and bandwidth. If your business uses a cloud provider, you can literally do this overnight. We call that *scalability*. If your business needs to expand or reduce its network capacity, everything can be scaled up or down quickly. Cloud providers typically have millions of server machines in multiple datacenters around the world, and they're managing the networks of possibly millions of businesses and organizations. They could be large, multibillion-dollar corporations like Disney, or small businesses with five people and annual revenues of $500,000. Businesses of all sizes and industries have benefited from the power of the cloud.

There are two basic ways your business can implement a cloud provider. You could have a hybrid cloud network, with some servers on your premises integrated with the part of your network that's managed by your cloud provider. Or you could just have a LAN and endpoints, and all of your servers are managed by your cloud provider. Your IT professionals can help you decide what's best for your organization's needs.

Implementing a cloud network is an effective way to build the resilience and redundancy you need so your business can thrive in the wake of cyberattacks and accidental incidents. It's incredibly difficult to make a successful denial-of-service attack on Amazon Web Services (AWS), for example, because its infrastructure is just that huge. Cloud providers build redundancy into your own systems, so if one server or data storage device fails, there are many others with the same data and applications.

Regardless of whether your business uses a cloud provider, you should back up your data and applications locally, on your own premises. If you don't use a cloud provider, local backups and redundant servers on your premises are absolutely vital because you probably don't have a remote backup. If you do use a cloud provider, you will want to also back your data up locally in case something happens to your access to the cloud provider. However, your cloud network may handle a lot more data than you have the local capacity to duplicate. In that case, you should use your local backup for your most crucial and mission-critical data and applications.

When it comes to cybersecurity and incident response when you are implementing a cloud provider, it's absolutely essential to understand which entity is responsible for what. If your network is entirely on your premises, then the responsibility is easy to understand. Your organization is responsible for everything. But if your organization uses a cloud provider, at least some of your data and applications are being managed by their servers and storage devices, in their own facilities, possibly hundreds or thousands of miles away from your workplace. How do you know who is responsible for what?

Your organization is responsible for your data in the cloud. If there are vulnerabilities in the applications or code you deploy through your cloud provider, whether your company developed it or whether it was developed by a third party, your organization is responsible if those vulnerabilities are exploited. That applies to all applications and code that wasn't authored by your cloud provider. If there are vulnerabilities in how your applications in the cloud are configured, that too is the responsibility of your organization. But major cloud providers such as AWS or Google Cloud Platform do provide many software tools for encrypting your data and applications, and they provide other kinds of software cybersecurity controls as well. Cloud providers make plenty of documentation available for your developers and network administrators to show them how to use the provider's security features properly. Also, you can often phone or email your cloud provider for support in using its security features. Over the course of my cybersecurity journalism career, I have reported on cyber incidents where companies had not used their cloud provider's security features properly. Don't repeat that common mistake. Make sure your security team uses every cloud provider security feature that's applicable according to how you use the cloud network.

Your cloud provider is responsible for the security of its infrastructure. If your data and applications are threatened due to the cloud provider's hardware failure or if the physical security of their infrastructure is threatened, that's on them. Make sure your security team reads all of your cloud provider's policies that explain what they're supposed to do if something goes wrong with their infrastructure and it harms the functioning of your organization's cloud network.

Back It Up, Back It Up, Back It Up

As long as you have full visibility and control of all of your organization's data, you can never have too many backups. Data can be stored in a variety of different media—hard disk drives, optical media (such as DVDs), flash media, even the good old-fashioned tape drives that have been used in datacenters since before I was born. These tape drives predated the early 1980s.

Make sure your data is backed up in as many places as possible, both on your premises and in the cloud, in places that your organization can control. As I mentioned, cloud backups won't help your company if something happens with the connection to your cloud network, so you should also have local backups.

As we have discussed, cyberattacks are a common threat to data in storage, but there other, much less sinister events can threaten your stored data too. Natural disasters such as floods, hurricanes, and tornados can do serious, often irreversible damage to computers and their data storage.

If your facilities experience an interruption in electrical power, that too can damage your computers and data storage. Your organization's on-premises network should have backup power that suits your budget and needs. This could be a backup power generator, a backup power fuel cell, or an uninterruptible power supply (UPS) if you have a small business, a small budget, and a small network. A UPS device, the least expensive and lowest capacity option, can be purchased for as little as $200. However, using one will increase your electrical power bills, so keep that in mind. Depending on what kind of backup power your local network has, different things can happen in the event of a power outage. You could have an extra hour of electricity that gives your IT department time to shut all of your computers down properly while protecting your data. Or with the highest capacity and most expensive backup power options, your business may be able to run your network for days without receiving electricity from your power grid.

Another threat to data in storage is the fact that disks don't last forever. Magnetic media hard disk drives (HDDs), the kind that have been commonly used in PCs for more than 30 years, seldom last longer than 30 years. Magnetic media will eventually deteriorate, as will newer technology flash media disks. Just to be safe, if any of your disk drives are older than 15 years or so, you should copy the data on those disks to new, recently manufactured disk drives. Yes, the data written onto HDDs in the 1980s and 1990s is now physically deteriorating as I write this, if they haven't physically failed already. Tim Berners-Lee invented the World Wide Web, and the first HTML written web pages were written by him in 1991, a historical monument. If that data hasn't already been backed up to drives that are newer than the one that was in Berners-Lee's NeXT computer, they'd be gone forever, no matter how carefully he could have handled them. *Periodically back up your crucial data to newer disk drives.*

RAID

Now it's time to get a little bit nerdy. This part will interest you if you enjoy learning about information technology. Let me introduce you to the wonderful world of RAID configurations.

RAID stands for *redundant arrays of inexpensive disks.* It's indeed a relatively inexpensive way to configure multiple disks in a way so that if one or more disks fail, you can still access your data. The term was invented by David Patterson, Garth A. Gibson, and Randy Katz at the University of California Berkeley in 1987. It's still a commonly used and effective data storage methodology today.

Here are some terms that will impress your IT department if you use them properly in conversation. There are three different ways that data can be written onto RAID drives: striping, parity, and mirroring.

Imagine the data on your RAID drive as if it were a book. In striping, some of the pages are on one disk, some are on another disk, and some are on the third disk, but no individual disk contains the entire book. To read the entire book, you will need all the disks in the RAID configuration.

Parity is kind of like the table of contents. If you're missing pages of the book, it'll help to show you which pages you're missing, but the parity data doesn't contain the actual content of the book.

Mirroring is exactly what it sounds like. The entire book is on each and every disk. The data on each disk should be identical to the data on any of the other disks.

In a RAID 0 configuration, data is allocated between the disks with striping only. You will lose some data if a single disk fails. The only major advantage to a RAID 0 configuration is that data can be read and written fast, because the data that could be written all on one disk is scattered among multiple disks. But with the advent of flash media HDDs, RAID 0's main selling point has largely become obsolete. Data can be read and written off of flash media faster than it can from magnetic media.

RAID 1 is rock-solid. In a RAID 1 configuration, all the disks are mirrored. This is my personal favorite RAID configuration, because if any individual disk fails, you don't lose any data. Without knowing the specifics of your data storage situation, I would recommend RAID 1 to your IT department if you're able to do it.

You'll probably never see RAID 2 these days. No RAID device vendors support it anymore. It was a RAID configuration that used parity and striping. Data would be striped onto multiple disks in sequential order: if page 1 was on the first disk, then page 2 was on the second, and so forth.

You might see RAID 3 these days, but it's seldom used. It uses parity and striping in a way that's similar to RAID 2. You probably don't want me to bore you with the details.

RAID 4 also uses parity and striping. It's uncommon but more frequently seen than RAID 2 or 3. In RAID 4, there's a parity disk and two striped disks. The main difference compared to RAID 2 and 3 is some really nerdy input/output technicalities. I'll spare you, as this book isn't a technical manual.

RAID 5 requires at least five disks, but that's not why it's called that. Parity and striped data is written on all of the disks. The parity is implemented in such a way that you don't lose data if one disk fails. If more than one disk fails, though, you might be out of luck.

The final standard RAID level is RAID 6. This is a striping and parity system that needs at least four disks, but the more you can use the better. It has a fault tolerance of two disks. In my opinion, it's the second-best standard RAID configuration, but use RAID 1 if you can. That way, every single drive would have to fail for you to lose data.

If you have a small business, there are inexpensive external drive bays that you can buy (some being approximately $50). Some of these could even fit onto your desk in the office. You could put four or six HDDs in these external bays, even if the HDDs were designed to be installed inside of your computer. These external bays usually support some RAID configurations. This is an excellent way to back up your data locally, especially if your organization is small.

On the much larger end of the spectrum, there are RAID devices that are designed for rackmounts in datacenters. These things are enormous but useful if you have a large enterprise that can support an on-premises datacenter.

What Ransomware Taught Business About Backups

Recall that ransomware is malware that encrypts your data without giving you access to the decryption key. Instead, a ransom note will appear on your computer screen in the form of a text document, a local web page, or something similar. The ransom note will be obvious, because cyberattackers want you to see it. In the note, they will tell you that you cannot get your data back unless you pay them a hefty ransom—perhaps $20,000 to $100,000 or more in cryptocurrency.

If your organization hasn't backed up your data on a disk the ransomware can't access, then it may be lost forever if you don't pay the attacker's expensive fee. Although in some ransomware attacks, attackers may not decrypt your data even if your organization does pay the ransom.

The major downside to paying the ransom, other than the expense, is that your company may be playing a role in showing cybercriminals that ransomware is a profitable form of cybercrime, encouraging them to do it more.

In the 2000s, ransomware typically targeted Windows consumers and demanded credit card numbers. More recently, cyberattackers have realized that businesses and enterprises are more profitable victims, so those entities have become the main ransomware target.

Organizations that haven't been backing their data up properly learned the hard way when ransomware hit their networks. If you have good backups, your company can choose to not pay the ransom. Just thumb your nose at the cybercriminal and restore data from your backups instead.

When the WannaCry ransomware hit in 2017, it was the most destructive ransomware to date. Large numbers of companies around the world learned from that incident, and proper backups became more common everywhere.

So, you might think that all you have to do is back up all of your company's data, and then you won't have to worry about ransomware anymore. I have bad news for you.

Sometimes organizations have had backups but have chosen to pay the ransom anyway. I reported on a SamSam ransomware attack for BlackBerry Cylance's blog in February 2018. In "Hospital Had Backups, Paid Ransom Anyway," I wrote:

> On January 11th, Hancock Regional Hospital in Indiana discovered that their computers had been infected with SamSam ransomware, a malware variant which has existed since early 2016. The hospital decided to pay the four Bitcoin ransom in order to get their files decrypted, which was worth around $55,000 USD at the time.
>
> I know what you must be thinking. "Here's another institution which couldn't recover from a cyberattack properly because they didn't bother to keep backups!" No, they had backups.

The gist of Hancock Regional Hospital's problem is that restoring data from their backups would have taken too long. Hospitals need immediate and constant access to their data. Not having access to a patient's data quickly enough in a hospital setting could negatively impact patient health. Which prescriptions are they on? What allergies do they have? Which procedures were done to them? What's their medical condition? Who's treating them? Because Hancock Regional Hospital couldn't recover from its backups quickly enough, it paid the ransom.

Especially if you have a large network, make sure that you test how quickly you can recover backup data in the event of a cyber incident or similar emergency.

Here's another issue that I've mentioned before. Because organizations became less likely to pay ransoms due to keeping better backups, emerging ransomware strains from the past couple of years have threatened to breach sensitive data to the public or to cybercriminals if a company doesn't pay the ransom quickly enough. You absolutely should back up as much of your data as possible and test your backups, but that alone won't mitigate this new threat. You will need to prevent ransomware infections in the first place through different security controls.

If your network runs Windows servers, one of the best ways you can prevent ransomware infections is to disable Windows Remote Desktop Protocol (RDP) if at all possible. Most (but not all) Windows ransomware infects machines through RDP. It is preferable for your network administrator to find an alternative way to remotely administrate Windows machines. Do keep in mind, however, that disabling RDP doesn't guarantee that your network won't be hit by ransomware; it makes it only less likely. You should also deploy regularly updated antivirus systems throughout your network and also engage in other network security principles, such as disabling any TCP/IP ports you don't use. If this isn't your area of expertise, your IT department and security team should take care of this.

Ultimately, you can never eliminate the risk of cyber threats. You can only make them less likely to harm your network or do less damage. Nothing is ever 100 percent secure.

Business Continuity

I've covered the importance of creating data backups and making sure you can recover from them. Now let's get into a related but broader topic: business continuity. Having a business continuity plan is essential to making sure your company can thrive in the wake of dangerous threats. Cyberattacks are just one of those threats. You will also have to make sure your business can continue when other sorts of threats strike.

The Covid-19 pandemic is an excellent example of something that isn't a cyberattack but that can have a catastrophic effect on business if you don't plan properly. You spend many years and possibly millions of dollars building your business. It would be a shame to see what you worked so hard to build disintegrate due to a lack of preparedness.

Business continuity planning is one facet of cybersecurity, even though it also constitutes parts of your business that are unrelated to computers. Let's go over the basics so your company can start planning right away.

Consider all the insurance options that could be applicable to your business. Contact insurance brokers that specialize in the various forms of insurance for commercial entities. You could consider fire, accident, and natural disaster insurance. Insurance plans could financially compensate your business if something terrible happens, but make sure the benefits of an insurance plan are worth it relative to your monthly premiums and the details of the plan. Keep in mind that a business insurance policy may only cover loss or damage to your inventory and equipment. If you're unsure about this, a lawyer or an industry-specific organization could offer you advice.

Insurance alone is never enough. It may take time to receive insurance benefits in the event of an emergency, and your insurance company won't be doing the work of keeping your business running.

Sit down with your security team to figure out how your business can continue to operate during a variety of different events. What if ransomware hits all your computers? What if your workplace has a significant fire? What if a natural disaster hits your workplace? Consider all the possibilities and plan accordingly. Your plans will be unique to the specifics of your business, including how and where it operates. This is like planning for cyber incident response, but broader because it should also cover bad stuff that has nothing to do with cyber incidents. Yes, "bad stuff" is the technical term.

Disaster Recovery

People often confuse business continuity and disaster recovery. Disaster recovery is a component of business continuity planning. Business continuity involves making sure your business can continue operation during disasters and many other significant events. Disaster recovery is all about making sure your business can survive natural disasters. You can think of business continuity as your plans to keep running, and disaster recovery as your plan for what to do in the aftermath of a disaster, including how to recover from it. Business continuity is running laps around the track; disaster recovery is what you get when you've crossed the finish line—a towel to wipe up your sweat and a bottle of water to replenish your lost fluids.

First, you need to consider which sorts of natural disasters affect the geography of your workplace. Japan and Southern California are susceptible to intense earthquakes. Places near rivers and the shores of the Gulf of Mexico are susceptible to flooding. Most of the middle of the continental United States is susceptible to tornadoes. Florida is susceptible to hurricanes. Chances are that the location of your workplace is susceptible to some type of natural disaster. Keep in mind, climate change is making natural disasters worldwide more frequent and destructive. "Once in a lifetime" storms are now becoming annual events. The importance of having robust disaster recovery plans is greater now than ever.

Government agencies have websites that are full of information about how to prepare for disasters in your area. Most of the information is geared toward individuals and families at home, but a lot of the information can also be applied to businesses and institutions. Certainly, saving your computers and business systems is good, but saving human lives should be prioritized over everything else. Your organization should share disaster and emergency preparation and resources with your employees and contractors so that everyone can have the best chance for survival when something unexpected happens.

If you're in the United States, check out the US government website `www.ready.gov` for information specific to your area. The equivalent from the Canadian government is `www.getprepared.gc.ca`. The European Union has the Disaster Risk Management Knowledge Centre available at `https://drmkc.jrc.ec.europa.eu`.

If your country is somewhere else in the world, doing a web search for your country's name and *disaster preparedness* should return useful results.

The Covid-19 pandemic has taught me that a lot of people will not take life-or-death emergencies seriously, and they will behave in ways that harm other people. I've seen way too many people enter retail stores without their masks or with their nose poking out of their mask. I've even heard of the many "anti-mask" protests in major city centers. I think the lesson to be learned here is to be mentally and emotionally prepared for people to disregard others' safety. As a business leader, you should make it clear to everyone who reports to you that you have zero tolerance for people who don't take the safety of your staff and customers seriously. You should even consider terminating the employment of someone who refuses to cooperate with disaster safety policies and procedures.

Disaster preparedness should include making sure each of your workplaces has at least one fully stocked first-aid kit. You should probably have multiple first-aid kits if your workplace supports more than 100 employees or contractors. A proper first-aid kit should have a wide assortment of bandages, topical antibacterial ointments such as polysporin, and analgesics such as ibuprofen and aspirin. If you don't have time to assemble first-aid kits yourself, most major pharmacy chains stock ready-made first-aid kits in multiple sizes. Make sure to replace over time any first-aid kit components that are used. Some jurisdictions make it illegal for an employee to give fellow employees drugs like aspirin directly. In that case, find a way that your employees can take those drugs in a lawful way, perhaps by keeping the first-aid kit accessible for them to take it themselves.

You should also make sure as many of your employees as possible are trained in first aid and cardiopulmonary resuscitation (CPR). Your area's Red Cross or St. John Ambulance organization may be able to offer first-aid and CPR training for your employees and executives. Making sure your workplace always has people who can provide first aid saves lives. If you have the resources for it, you should also consider providing an automated external defibrillator (AED) for your workplace. The organizations I mentioned can also help you find a retailer of AED devices, but it is important that your employees are trained in how to use one properly.

A fire could also threaten the safety of employees and customers at any sort of workplace. Contact your local fire department for help with creating a fire escape plan and with making sure you have fire extinguishers on-site. Your fire department can also help you to evaluate your workplace to make it safer. For instance, unsafe electrical wiring can be a major fire risk. You should also make sure your workplace has plenty of smoke detectors and carbon monoxide detectors and that their batteries are changed at least twice per year. Carbon monoxide leaks are invisible and have no odor, so a carbon monoxide detector is the only way you'll know if this deadly gas is leaking in your facility.

Once you can ensure the safety of your employees, the next step is to protect your business. The pandemic has shown us that many companies can support people working from home. If your employees and contractors can work from home, you should facilitate that. It certainly is helpful for disabled workers and workers with childcare and eldercare responsibilities at home. An added benefit is some extra resilience in the wake of a natural disaster. Think about it this way: if all of your office staff work from cubicles in one building, they'd all be impacted if a tornado hit it. But if your office staff work from a multitude of different home offices, it's unlikely that the same tornado would impact all of them.

Sometimes a disaster can attack an entire city or your employees have to work from one building due to the nature of your business. For instance, restaurant workers can't work from home. What can you do then? Disaster recovery introduces the concept of hot sites, warm sites, and cold sites as possible backup workplaces in the event of a disaster. These sites should be in a different but nearby city from where your usual workplace is. That way, the backup site is less likely to be hit by the same disaster as your main site, but your workers can still commute to it if the need arises. Finding backup sites about 30 kilometers or 20 miles away from your main site is ideal.

A hot site is a backup workplace that can be used immediately. To be ready right away, it needs to run continuously even when you're not using it. That includes electrical power, network connectivity, and all the necessary on-site computers and equipment. All the computer data you have in your main workplace should also be regularly backed up to the computers in your hot site. Hot sites are great for making sure that there's minimal interruption to your business continuity, but it's also expensive because you have to keep paying your utility bills for the site, and you may need to maintain some physical security and IT staff for it.

A warm site is a less expensive option. You still need to keep electrical power and network connectivity running constantly and ensure all the computers and equipment you need are ready at the site, but you may not be backing up data or having staff check the site regularly like you would for a hot site. Continuing work from a warm site will take more time than with a hot site, and it will interrupt your business a bit longer, while costing your company less money.

A cold site is the least expensive type of backup workplace. You don't have to keep electricity and internet running at a cold site when it's not in use. You may have some tables, chairs, and equipment, but you wouldn't have everything you need for business operation at your cold site. Restoring and resuming business from a cold site will take the longest, but if it's the best your budget can support, it's better than having no backup workplace at all.

If it's not possible for your organization to have a backup workplace, you will need to factor that into your disaster recovery plans. As you design your disaster recovery plans, be thorough and prepare for every possible contingency, even if the likelihood of the contingency occurring is low. There's an old adage: a stitch in time saves nine.

Building resilience in your company's computer network and preparing for accidents and disasters requires a bit of planning. Your organization should also properly budget for it.

You'll find all of this effort and investment is worth it, because you never know what might happen to your data and your business. If you act properly, $20,000 and a couple of days' worth of preparation could save your business $2,000,000 and multiple weeks of recovery.

Take full advantage of cloud providers, backup electricity, employee training, and government disaster resources. With this step taken care of, you'll be well on your way to having a cyber threat– and natural threat–ready business.

Chapter 9
Afterword

Now, you've read all about my *8 Steps to Better Security*. This is my methodology to make sure your business is off to a good start when it comes to thriving in the evolving cyber threat landscape.

Let's review the most important ideas in each of the eight steps. I also recommend other books to further your understanding of the topics I've covered.

Step 1

The foundation of being a cyber-resilient business is to foster a strong security culture. This is where you must always start. Cybersecurity is primarily a social phenomenon, contrary to popular belief. You absolutely must have people who understand how to securely deploy, implement, configure, and maintain computer technology. Having people with technical skills on your security team is important, but all the information technology and computer science skills in the world are useless without the right attitude and culture to support their proper use.

Your company's security culture is the way everyone in your organization behaves relative to cybersecurity. It's something that must be developed and nurtured over time. Like everything else in cybersecurity, it's not something you can set and forget (like a cheesy infomercial). Security is a process. Think of it as a houseplant that requires everyday care.

Let's summarize the ideas I introduced in step 1.

The Most Notorious Cyberattacker Was Actually a Con Man

Kevin Mitnick is famous for his cyberattacks in the 1980s and 1990s. He is perhaps the first individual cyberattacker to become really well known in the media. A layperson may assume that Mitnick was a master computer scientist, but the truth is that his infamous cyber exploits didn't require advanced technical skill. He was an old-fashioned con man. He made news headlines for penetrating the networks of DEC and Pacific Bell. But he managed to do it mainly by tricking employees into giving him authentication credentials. In a cybersecurity context, we call these *social engineering* attacks.

The moral of the Kevin Mitnick story is that human psychology and sociology represent a major facet of cybersecurity. Even in the 2020s, most cyberattacks involve social engineering at one point or another.

A Strong Security Culture Requires All Hands on Deck

Fostering a strong security culture doesn't stop at your IT department. Absolutely everyone in your organization must be a part of it. Even a janitor who never directly interacts with your computer network has physical access to your computers that a cyberattacker may want to exploit.

Hackers Are the Good Guys, Actually

The original hackers were the people who invented some of the computer technology you use every day: the Linux kernel (found primarily in Android and internet servers), the TCP/IP foundation of the modern internet, the open-source code in your web browser, and so forth. Being a hacker is all about finding novel and innovative ways to use computer technology.

Unfortunately, the general public seems to believe that the word *hacker* is a synonym for *cyberattacker*. Many people in the cybersecurity community self-identify as hackers. Promoting the correct usage of the word *hacker* will likely make you more popular with cybersecurity professionals, and happy cybersecurity professionals can greatly improve your organization's cyber resilience.

What Is Security Culture?

J. Wolfgang Goerlich, Duo Security Advisory CISO of Cisco Systems, probably has the best description of what security culture is:

> Security culture comes from a partnership between security champions and security advocates. A security advocate is a member of the security team who focuses on getting practices into the hands of the workforce. It's more common for us to talk about security champions. A security champion is a member of the business itself, who collaborates with the security team on best practices. A culture of security has advocates working with champions to interpret and implement security controls. In a well-run security practice, controls will be usable and widely adopted because of the partnership of advocates and champions.
>
> All security controls are useless if it is ignored. Good security is usable security. Good security is adopted security. The starting point, then, is empathy and kindness for the people we are charged with defending.

My tip for fostering a strong security culture is to deploy frequent security training in your organization for all of your workers. Make it fun and engaging. Place a special emphasis on training people to resist social engineering, such as phishing and Trojan malware.

What Makes a Good CISO?

Not all organizations have a chief information security officer (CISO). But if your business has the resources to support one, they can be an extremely valuable asset, leading your security team and being a liaison with the nontechnical members of your C-suite.

Mitch Parker is a CISO who had an excellent response to my question about what makes a good CISO:

> This question in itself has had entire books written about it. However, the answer is a lot simpler than people make it out to be. This position requires people who are able to effectively communicate and present, assess, and address risks, and develop plans to improve the security maturity of the organization. The goals of security are aligned with continual quality improvement. Focusing on the overall organizational goals and aligning with existing quality improvement initiatives to reduce risk and improve overall business processes while effectively communicating and updating the team is what makes a good CISO. The rest is semantics and mechanics.

The Psychological Phases of a Cybersecurity Professional

As you build your security team, it will help you to understand the different psychological phases that many of my peers and I have observed:

- **Phase 1**: Now I've got all this technical cybersecurity knowledge. Let's make everything 100 percent secure.
- **Phase 2**: A cybersecurity professional learns that nothing can be made 100 percent secure. Computer technology is increasingly complex, and sometimes implementing security controls that are too strict makes computers impractical to use, which can definitely hurt your company's productivity. But the cybersecurity professionals get stuck on the idea that the biggest security problem is their foolish, ignorant users. Unfortunately, some cybersecurity professionals stay stuck in this phase forever. I was at that phase until a few years ago.
- **Phase 3**: Wiser cybersecurity professionals learn that all human beings are fallible, including themselves. Even the most adept technicians can make careless mistakes with technology. Good security design considers human nature. A prime example of

this occurred when sensitive information was displayed on computer monitors during the US Capitol attack of January 2021. Do you expect people to calmly shut down their PCs while they have to flee to avoid deadly gunfire? Or do you design your network to automatically shut down PCs during an emergency evacuation order? The latter is the much more practical solution.

Recommended Readings

The Cybersecurity Playbook: How Every Leader and Employee Can Contribute to a Culture of Security

Author: Allison Cerra
Publisher: Wiley Tech
Pages: 224
ISBN: 978-1-119-44213-4
Link: `https://www.wiley.com/en-ca/The+Cybersecurity+Playbook%3A+How+Every+Leader+and+Employee+Can+Contribute+to+a+Culture+of+Security-p-9781119442134`

Cerra's book is a great way to learn more about fostering a strong security culture in your organization. In a similar way to my book (the one you're reading right now), Cerra gives you a step-by-step guide to the constant, everyday process of security culture. She understands that it requires the work of everyone in your organization.

Transformational Security Awareness: What Neuroscientists, Storytellers, and Marketers Can Teach Us About Driving Secure Behaviors

Author: Perry Carpenter
Publisher: Wiley Tech
Pages: 368
ISBN: 978-1-119-56635-9
Link: `https://www.wiley.com/en-ca/Transformational+Security+Awareness%3A+What+Neuroscientists%2C+Storytellers%2C+and+Marketers+Can+Teach+Us+About+Driving+Secure+Behaviors-p-9781119566359`

Perry's approach emphasizes the psychological and neuroscientific aspects of fostering a strong security culture. This book will teach you how to design and deploy an effective security awareness program that's best suited to your organization's needs.

Step 2

The next step is to build a strong security team. This process may differ according to the size of your company and its industry. A small business may have only one person doing IT work. (A small business may have only one person using one computer.) By default, that person is your security team. A large corporation, on the other hand, can hire a security team of hundreds of people, which will include defensive and offensive security specialists.

In this step, I challenge some conventional wisdom about hiring cybersecurity professionals.

Tackling the Cybersecurity Skills Gap Myth

The supposed "cybersecurity skills gap" illustrates the mindset conflict between the business community and the actual security practitioners.

According to this myth, millions of cybersecurity roles in companies around the world are left vacant because job applicants have a deficit. People simply don't have the advanced cybersecurity skills that businesses need in the 21st century, so companies cannot find the right people to hire. This may be the fault of job applicants or schools, or a combination of the two.

This myth is incredibly dangerous. Here's what my friends in the cybersecurity industry and I have observed: job postings have unrealistic expectations.

Sometimes they significantly underpay for credentials and experience that cost lots of money to acquire and take many years in the industry to earn. A heart surgeon with seven years of medical school won't work for $40,000 per year, so why do companies expect people with advanced cybersecurity certifications and many years of experience to work for such low pay?

Other expectations in job postings are also wildly unreasonable. They can demand ten years of experience with a programming language that has existed for only five years. They can expect a network administrator to perform every single IT department and software development role. The list goes on.

The continuation of the cybersecurity skills gap myth has devastating effects. First, many crucial cybersecurity roles are being left vacant, weakening an organization's security posture. Second, the few cybersecurity professionals an organization has may be overburdened by being expected to perform the roles of many more people. They will perform poorly under so much stress, and they may leave for the sake of their mental health. Finally, lots of excellent cybersecurity professionals are left unemployed or underemployed because employers tend to nitpick.

A strong security team includes younger people and older people at different stages of their careers. The older people can mentor younger people, and younger people provide fresh thinking and will become your organization's seasoned cybersecurity professionals as the years go on.

If a job applicant doesn't have all the qualifications but they can demonstrate talent, train them. Spend money on their education. Help them prepare for and write cybersecurity certification exams. This investment in your people will make your organization's security posture much stronger. Happy employees will stay with your company, rather than take their new skills elsewhere. Give people a chance.

Take "Culture Fit" Out of Your Vocabulary

Human resources departments, especially in places like Silicon Valley, often expect for new hires to be a "culture fit" in their organization. Unfortunately, this kind of thinking often results in homogeneous security teams that lack sufficient diversity for cyber resilience. Too many companies favor white, cisgender men in their 20s, for example. (It's okay to hire some white, cisgender young men, but they shouldn't be the entirety of your security team.) Just as you should be open-minded about hiring people from 18 to 60, you should also be open to hiring people of all races, ethnicities, and cultures; disabled people; LGBTQ people; and so on. Cybersecurity is a human practice, and a diversity of humans is naturally more effective at addressing the security needs of a diverse population.

Your Cybersecurity Budget

Cybersecurity budgets can vary greatly, depending on how large your company is, how large your network is, and which industry you're in. As a baseline, cybersecurity should be at least 3 percent to 5 percent of your overall IT budget, and perhaps 10 percent to 15 percent of your IT budget if you're in a security-sensitive industry such as financial services or healthcare.

Recommended Readings

Hiring for Diversity: The Guide to Building an Inclusive and Equitable Organization

Author: Arthur Woods
Publisher: Wiley Tech
Pages: 256
ISBN: 978-1-119-80090-3
Link: `https://www.wiley.com/en-ca/Hiring+for+Diversity%3A+The+Guide+to+Building+an+Inclusive+and+Equitable+Organization-p-9781119800903`

> Woods understands the importance of hiring a diverse team perhaps even better than I do. His book will help you refine and improve your hiring and employee retention procedures, improve your organization's accessibility, and shift your company's mindset when it comes to diverse and inclusive hiring.

Talent Makers: How the Best Organizations Win through Structured and Inclusive Hiring

Authors: Daniel Chait and Jon Stross

Publisher: Wiley Tech

Pages: 272

ISBN: 978-1-119-78528-6

Link: `https://www.wiley.com/en-ca/Talent+Makers%3A+How+the+Best+Organizations+Win+through+Structured+and+Inclusive+Hiring-p-9781119785286`

> Chait and Stross's book is a must read, not only when it comes to hiring for cybersecurity but also for hiring in all areas of your organization. This guide is full of actionable strategies for improving diversity, equity, and inclusion in your company, regardless of your industry.

Step 3

Regulatory compliance is an absolute must. There are many data security regulations that can apply to your company, depending on where in the world you operate and which industry you're in. Making sure you comply with these regulations is critical. Violating a regulation can result in millions of dollars of fines and damage your company's reputation. But remember that regulatory compliance shouldn't be your security baseline. Your organization should go above and beyond your legal and regulatory security requirements.

Data Breaches

Data breaches are one of the most common types of security incidents your organization will face. Exposing sensitive data can give cybercriminals control of your computer network and your company. Plus, you need to keep your financial data and research and development information private for the sake of your company's bottom line.

If your company's data breach becomes public knowledge, it will greatly harm your company's reputation. Customers, clients, and other companies will be less likely to want to do business with you. Plus, data breaches can result in massive regulatory fines and very expensive litigation.

According to IBM's 2020 Cost of a Data Breach Study, the average data breach in the United States costs $8.64 million. Data breaches are much more common than the media may have you believe, and many go undetected for a long time. Security hardening against data breaches should be one of your company's top priorities.

Data Privacy Regulations

There are too many data privacy regulations worldwide for me to describe in this book, but here are some of the more common regulations you should know about.

The General Data Protection Regulation (GDPR) is European Union legislation. If your company is in the EU, you definitely need to comply with it, but even if your company is outside of Europe, the GDPR can pertain to your company's network if you ever handle data about an EU citizen or entity. So many companies in the Americas, Africa, Asia, and Oceania also need to worry about GDPR compliance.

The California Consumer Privacy Act (CCPA) is modeled on the GDPR. It pertains to Californian data that isn't covered by American financial and medical data regulations. Like the GDPR, it applies to not only businesses in California but also businesses outside of California that handle data on Californian people and entities.

The Health Insurance Portability and Accountability Act (HIPAA) applies to all American personal health data, both digital and printed on paper. Medical clinics, medical practitioners, hospitals, and health insurance companies in the United States need to be concerned about it.

The Gramm-Leach-Bliley Act pertains to American financial data. This is mainly a concern of the US financial services industry rather than the nonfinancial retail sector. These regulations can be highly complex and if you're an American credit union, bank, mortgage broker, creditor, or money lender, or if you work in the stock market, you should definitely find a lawyer who specializes in financial regulations to advise you about compliance.

The Payment Card Industry Data Security Standard (PCI DSS) pertains to the security of debit cards and credit cards. It's an international regulation. It's enforced by the Payment Card Industry Security Standards Council, a collective of many financial service providers including Visa, MasterCard, and American Express. Your retail (online or offline) or food service business will not be allowed to accept credit card or debit card payment without PCI DSS compliance. And their fines can be pretty hefty.

When your business acquires a point-of-sale system, you'll probably get documentation about PCI DSS compliance. Read it and make sure you're compliant.

Risk Management

In cybersecurity, there's no such thing as zero risk. One of the keys to maintaining a strong security posture is proper risk assessment and management.

Threat modeling is about anticipating risk and danger and acting in a way to mitigate it. It involves thinking about what bad things can happen and what you will do to prevent them from happening or to reduce their harm. For example, cyberattackers will send your employees email with malware. You can train your employees to avoid opening email attachments from people they don't know. You can also install antivirus software on their PC endpoints and on your email server.

Recommended Readings

Solving Cyber Risk: Protecting Your Company and Society

Authors: Andrew Coburn, Eireann Leverett, and Gordon Woo
Publisher: Wiley Tech
Pages: 384
ISBN: 978-1-119-49092-0
Link: `https://www.wiley.com/en-ca/Solving+Cyber+Risk%3A+Protecting+Your+Company+and+Society-p-9781119490920`

This book goes into detail about risk management for cybersecurity. It'll help you understand what motivates cyberattackers, where the most damaging types of cyber loss occur, and how to properly manage your cybersecurity resources.

Privacy, Regulations, and Cybersecurity: The Essential Business Guide

Author: Chris Moschovitis
Publisher: Wiley Tech
Pages: 416
ISBN: 978-1-119-66011-8
Link: `https://www.wiley.com/en-ca/Privacy%2C+Regulations%2C+and+Cybersecurity%3A+The+Essential+Business+Guide-p-9781119660118`

Because my book covers all areas of business cybersecurity in general, I could only introduce the concept of data privacy regulations. Moschovitis' book goes into much more detail. Understanding the regulations that apply to your business and compliance with them is absolutely essential, so you should check this book out.

Step 4

Your computer network will constantly grow and change. For that reason, frequent security testing is essential. With that information, your security team can security-harden your organization.

Security Audits

Security audits are conducted by regulatory bodies and government agencies. They'll test your security according to a specific standard, such as the HIPAA regulation. Your company can't always predict when a security audit will be conducted. So, you must security test your own network and assure regulatory compliance.

Vulnerability Assessments

A vulnerability assessment is a way to find as many vulnerabilities in your organization as you can, in a generalized way. The assessment will provide your organization with a report on which vulnerabilities are the most urgent to address and how to remedy them. They're a good idea regardless of your company's security maturity, size, or industry.

Vulnerability assessments can be conducted based on checklists of traits your network and organization should have. For example, do you have security cameras on your doors? Do you have any internet ports that are open without a good reason? Do you patch your software regularly?

Penetration Testing

Only organizations with a higher security maturity level should be penetration tested. During a penetration test, security professionals will simulate cyberattacks to your company and your network. If they can penetrate your network like a cyberattacker, you can find security problems that must be addressed.

One of the reasons why pentests aren't appropriate for all organizations is because if you haven't passed many vulnerability assessments and if your security isn't robust, a pentest can damage your company and find way too many vulnerabilities for a pentester to work with. Plus, your company may not be able to implement a penetration tester's findings. Your organization should wait until you've seriously worked on your cybersecurity for years before you conduct your first pentest.

Bug Bounty Programs

A bug bounty program is offered to the general public to find security vulnerabilities in the software your company develops. They're kind of like an application penetration test open to the outside world. For that reason, your organization should have a bug bounty program only if your company develops software, has a high level of security maturity, and has the infrastructure and resources to handle thousands of software exploits and triage thousands of bug reports. Large tech companies like Microsoft and Apple are perfect examples of organizations that can benefit from bug bounty programs. Your indie development house of 20 people shouldn't have a bug bounty program.

Recommended Reading

Corporate Cybersecurity: Identifying Risks and the Bug Bounty Program

Author: John Jackson
Publisher: Wiley Tech
Pages: 220
ISBN: 978-1-119-78252-0
Link: https://www.wiley.com/en-ca/Corporate+Cybersecurity%3A+Identifying+Risks+and+the+Bug+Bounty+Program-p-9781119782520

> Depending on when you've purchased my book, Jackson's book may not be published yet. But he's my friend, and we've discussed his book together. If your company is considering implementing a bug bounty program, this is the best guide to help you get started. Bug bounty programs can greatly improve the security of your software, but only if you conduct your bug bounty program the right way. This book will help you get your bug bounty program right the first time.

Penetration Testing for Dummies

Author: Robert Shimonski
Publisher: Wiley Tech
Pages: 256
ISBN: 978-1-119-57746-1
Link: https://www.wiley.com/en-ca/Penetration+Testing+For+Dummies-p-9781119577461

> Shimonski's book is designed for people who are interested in the penetration testing field. But there's also a lot of useful information here for businesses that are ready to start pentesting. This book can even help you figure out if you need pentesting in the first place or if you should stick with vulnerability assessments for now. Everything here is easy to understand in plain English.

Step 5

Cybersecurity frameworks can be the foundation of your company's cyber incident response program.

Incident Response

Incident response is your organization's plan to manage inevitable cyber incidents. First, you must prepare for your incident response. There must be company funding and approval for all the details of your incident response plan.

You must train your defensive security specialists to respond to cyber incidents. This includes detecting possible indications of compromise in your computer network and reacting quickly and effectively to prevent incidents or mitigate their damage, depending on the situation.

When your defensive security specialists have reacted to an incident, your organization will need a plan to recover from them. This can include improving your security defenses, documenting the incident so your team can learn lessons from it, and having legal and public relations advice to protect your company from litigation and reputation damage.

Cybersecurity Frameworks

Many organizations prefer to base their incident response plan on a cybersecurity framework. Popular frameworks include the NIST Cybersecurity Framework, the ISO 27000 Cybersecurity Frameworks, CIS Controls, and the COBIT Cybersecurity Framework. You may base your incident response plan on multiple frameworks or no framework at all. A strong security team will advise you on what your most effective incident response strategy should be.

Recommended Reading

Cyber Breach Response That Actually Works: Organizational Approach to Managing Residual Risk

Author: Andrew Gorecki
Publisher: Wiley Tech
Pages: 320
ISBN: 978-1-119-67931-8
Link: `https://www.wiley.com/en-ca/Cyber+Breach+Response+That+Actually+Works%3A+Organizational+Approach+to+Managing+Residual+Risk-p-9781119679318`

> Your organization's cyber incident response and effective cyber investigation are crucial when it comes to making sure cyber incidents do as little damage as possible to your business. Gorecki's guide will help your company prepare for whatever the ever-evolving cyber threat landscape throws at you.

Step 6

Your organization's cybersecurity efforts are essentially about protecting your data. Your computers and network infrastructure are important, but their importance is based on the data that they handle.

The CIA Triad

All cyber threats pertain to one or more of the three aspects of your data represented by the CIA triad: confidentiality, integrity, and availability. Confidentiality is about making sure your data is available only to the entities that are permitted to have it. Integrity is about making sure that only authorized entities can alter your data. Availability is about making sure your computer data is available when it's needed.

Access Control

Access control systems make sure that only authorized parties can access your data. There are many different ways to implement access control. Your choice of access control systems will vary according to your industry, your specific data needs, and possibly regulatory compliance.

Discretionary access control, mandatory access control, role-based access control, and attribute-based access control are some of the more common access control systems.

Patch Management

The software used for operating systems, applications, and hardware needs to be frequently updated to maintain good security. Security testers and software developers frequently discover security vulnerabilities in their software, and they develop code to patch those vulnerabilities.

Your organization needs to make sure that all your software receives all of its security patches when they become available. This isn't always as simple as it sounds, because patching can require internet access and rebooting your computers. You need a patch management system that assures your software is well patched while maintaining your company's operations.

Physical Security

Physical security is often overlooked, but it mustn't be. Your organization must make sure that only authorized entities have physical access to your computers. A cybercriminal can do a lot of harm if they can walk into your datacenter or office.

Important physical security controls include door locks, security guards and receptionists, and security cameras.

Malware

Malware is all malicious software. There are many different kinds of malware your organization should be worried about. Ransomware can maliciously encrypt your company's data and demand an expensive cryptocurrency ransom for decryption. Recent strains of malware have targeted institutions, and the enterprise can also threaten to breach your sensitive data to the general public. That's because companies are more likely to have effective data backups these days, so cybercriminals have found another extortion strategy.

Cryptominers can be malware if they're used on computers without their owner's consent. Cryptominers can cost your organization a lot of computing power and electricity, so that's why cryptomining malware should be avoided.

Spyware is a threat to data confidentiality, giving cybercriminals a means to breach your sensitive data.

Trojan malware can do many different malicious things. Their defining trait is how they pretend to be something a user wants in order to get them to interact with it. Malicious mobile apps and email attachments with filebinded malware are some of the most common examples of Trojans.

Cryptography

Cryptography is built into many of the computer technologies you use every day. Encryption is the application of cryptography, the means to protect data from cyber incidents pertaining to confidentiality and integrity.

The data that's transmitted through your network should be encrypted, as should your data in storage. There are different encryption standards for data in transit and data in storage. As much of your organization's data as possible should be encrypted.

BYOD and Working from Home

Bring your own device policies permit your employees to connect their own devices to your computer network, including phones and laptops. More and more organizations have people who are working from home, and the Covid-19 pandemic has accelerated this trend.

The commonality between bring your own device (BYOD) and work from home (WFH) is that they both introduce new cyberattack vectors to your computer network. Your security team should be mindful of this. Virtual private networks and antivirus software deployed to your workers' devices are important security controls in this realm.

Data Loss Prevention

A data leak occurs when sensitive data is exposed outside of your network, while your network still has the data. Data loss means that not only was your sensitive data breached to outside of your network, but your network actually lost the data.

There are data loss prevention (DLP) solutions that can prevent data leaks and data loss if your security team can configure these technologies properly.

Managed Service Providers

Managed service providers (MSPs) are all companies that manage various services for other companies to improve operations and cut expenses. There are MSPs that provide services that are specific to cybersecurity. If your company is a small business or a small or medium-sized enterprise (SME), you may need to hire an MSP.

Some cybersecurity services MSPs provide include authentication management, bandwidth management, intrusion detection and prevention, network administration, and data backup and recovery. Some MSPs can even provide your company with cloud network infrastructure.

Recommended Reading

Cryptography for Dummies
Author: Chey Cobb
Publisher: Wiley Tech
Pages: 324

ISBN: 978-0-764-56831-2
Link: https://www.wiley.com/en-ca/Cryptography+For+Dummies-p-9780764568312

> Cryptography is necessary to protect your company's data in transit and in storage. If you're not a computer nerd, Cobb's book is the perfect way to learn more about it. This is a great starting point to make sure your organization encrypts as much of your data as possible, and does so effectively.

Step 7

Cybersecurity is ultimately a human practice, so understanding the social factor is important to strengthening your organization's security posture.

Social Engineering

Social engineering is all about deceiving human beings. Most cyberattacks involve social engineering to at least some extent. Social engineering's psychological exploits long predate the invention of computers.

Trojan malware requires human interaction to execute. It can take the form of an application that the user believes will be a useful utility or a fun game. Or a Trojan can be an image or document with malware filebinded to it.

Phishing involves the use of emails, text messages, social media posts, or websites to imitate trusted entities in order to acquire sensitive data or access from their targets. Cybercriminals try to make sure that their malicious web pages, messages, or emails look legitimate. They could imitate your bank, your utility company, your social media platform, an entertainment platform, an online retailer, or a government agency. Phishing attacks are easier to execute than ever before because phishing kits can be purchased from the dark web that expertly imitate trusted entities. It's not only nontechnical people who are fooled by phishing; cybersecurity experts also sometimes succumb to phishing attacks. I try to avoid being a phishing victim by always visiting a company's website directly rather than clicking email links.

UI and UX Design

Good user interface (UI) and user experience (UX) design is important for cybersecurity. UI and UX affect how people interact with technology. Effective UX will show users how to use software in a secure way to avoid misuse through confusion and inconvenience.

Internal Threats

The harsh truth is that not all cyberattacks come from entities outside of your organization. Sometimes your employees and other stakeholders with authorized access to your computer network can conduct cyberattacks. In fact, internal cyberattacks can be easier to conduct than external cyberattacks because internal attackers already have authorized access.

Preventing internal cyberattacks requires a combination of conventional wisdom and my own possibly controversial unconventional wisdom. The conventional wisdom involves watching for disgruntled employees and for atypical employee behavior, such as unusual purchases or an eagerness to take on extra responsibilities. You also need to monitor your employee's user accounts through log analysis software and security information and event management systems (SIEMs) for user account behavior anomalies. That's all well and good, and I recommend all of that.

Here's my unconventional wisdom. One of the best ways you can prevent internal cyberattacks is to treat and pay your employees and contractors well. In my opinion, a happy employee is a loyal employee who is less likely to want to harm their employer. Plus, if they're well paid, they're less likely to be motivated to engage in "extracurricular activities" to make them extra money on the side through actions like cryptomining and selling sensitive company data.

Recommended Readings

The Art of Attack: Attacker Mindset for Security Professionals

Author: Maxie Reynolds
Publisher: Wiley Tech
Pages: 352
ISBN: 978-1-119-80546-5
Link: https://www.wiley.com/en-ca/The+Art+of+Attack%3A+Attacker+Mindset+for+Security+Professionals-p-9781119805465

> Reynolds' book is an excellent guide to furthering your understanding of the psychology of cyberattackers and how social engineering works. Thinking like an attacker is key to preventing cyberattacks to your organization.

Social Engineering: The Art of Human Hacking

Author: Christopher Hadnagy
Publisher: Wiley Tech
Pages: 416
ISBN: 978-0-470-63953-5
Link: https://www.wiley.com/en-ca/Social+Engineering%3A+The+Art+of+Human+Hacking-p-9780470639535

> Hadnagy is one of the top social engineering experts. His guide really goes in depth into the topic with a thorough understanding. As I've said, most cyberattacks involve social engineering at some point or another. Hadnagy also appreciates Kevin Mitnick's role in social engineering research.

Step 8

In the last step, your organization must build redundancy and resilience. This will assure that your company can weather storms—both literal and figurative.

Cloud Networks

Many organizations these days implement a cloud provider either as their entire computer network or as part of a hybrid with their on-premises network. One of the major advantages of cloud networks is their scalability. If your business needs a lot more data capacity and bandwidth or a lot less, you can ask your cloud provider to take care of that for you. It's a lot easier than buying or selling thousands of server machines and all of their necessary network infrastructure overnight.

Implementing a cloud network is a wonderful way to build the resilience and redundancy you need so your business can thrive in the wake of cyberattacks and accidental incidents. It's incredibly difficult to successfully conduct a denial-of-service attack on Amazon Web Services (AWS), for example, because its infrastructure is just that huge. Cloud providers build redundancy into your own systems, so if one server or data storage device fails, there are many others with the same data and applications.

When it comes to cybersecurity, it's important to understand who's responsible for what. Your cloud provider is responsible for the security of your cloud infrastructure. That includes keeping their hardware up and running and making sure only authorized parties have physical access to their datacenters. Your organization is responsible for the security of your data in the cloud. That includes implementing the security controls your cloud provider gives you, deploying secure application code, and monitoring your cloud data for cyber incidents.

Data Backups

Your organization must back up as much of your data as possible with local backups in addition to backups in your network. If an aspect of your network is hit by ransomware or some other sort of availability attack, you will need to have backups you can restore from quickly and effectively.

Redundancy is a good thing when it comes to your data. As long as you can maintain confidentiality and control, back up your data multiple times in as many places as you can.

Business Continuity and Disaster Recovery

Business continuity is all about making sure your business can continue operation during disasters and many other significant events. Disaster recovery is a component of business continuity planning. Disaster recovery involves making sure your business can survive natural disasters. Think of business continuity as your plans to keep the business running and disaster recovery as your plan for what to do in the aftermath of a disaster, including how to recover from it.

It's a good idea for your company to have specific business continuity plans. Are there alternative sites that your business can operate from if something unexpected happens to your primary work site? You also need your data and computer systems to be available in multiple places so your business can resume if something bad happens.

Disaster recovery planning requires an understanding of the types of natural disasters that can occur in your area. For instance, a business in San Francisco must prepare for earthquakes, and a business in Miami must prepare for hurricanes.

Government agencies have websites that are full of information about how to prepare for disasters in your area. Most of the information is geared to individuals and families at home, but a lot of the information can also be applied to businesses and institutions.

Recommended Readings

Faster Disaster Recovery: The Business Owner's Guide to Developing a Business Continuity Plan
Authors: Jennifer H. Elder and Samuel F. Elder
Publisher: Wiley Tech
Pages: 208
ISBN: 978-1-119-57094-3

Link: `https://www.wiley.com/en-ca/Faster+Disaster+Recovery%3A+The+Business+Owner%27s+Guide+to+Developing+a+Business+Continuity+Plan-p-9781119570943`

The Elders are business continuity and disaster recovery experts. Having a strong business continuity plan is essential because you must expect the unexpected in order for your organization to maintain resiliency. This book will help you prepare for disasters and other catastrophic events that are specific to your particular business.

Cloud Computing for Dummies
Authors: Judith S. Hurwitz and Daniel Kirsch
Publisher: Wiley Tech
Pages: 320
ISBN: 978-1-119-54677-1
Link: `https://www.wiley.com/en-ca/Cloud+Computing+For+Dummies%2C+2nd+Edition-p-9781119546771`

It's likely that your business will need to implement a cloud network. This book is the perfect guide to get you started, especially if you aren't a computer nerd. Here, you'll learn not only how to secure your data in the cloud but also how to leverage the cloud to improve your business overall.

Keeping Your Business Cyber Secure

Now that you've read all about my *8 Steps to Better Security*, you're on the right path to making sure your business can be cyber resilient. Effective cybersecurity begins with a strong security culture and team and is best implemented with proper security policies, procedures, training, and frequent security testing. Business cybersecurity is a broad topic that can be overwhelming. My goal with this book is to introduce business cybersecurity with an eight-step process that's easy to understand.

I recommend reviewing this book every so often to remember the various areas of business cybersecurity that apply to your organization. I've also recommended books that will expand upon the concepts I've covered in this book. *8 Steps to Better Security* is your starting point, but it's also where you can start to constantly reevaluate and reconceptualize your business' approach to cybersecurity.

All businesses in all industries need to be concerned about cybersecurity these days, because computer technology interacts with most of your company's functionality. I'm confident that you now have the right mindset to advance your business in this dynamic and volatile era. Remember that security is a constant process.

Index